THE FANTASY SPORTS BOSS 2014 FANTASY FOOTBALL DRAFT GUIDE

BY THE FANTASY SPORTS BOSS STAFF

TABLE OF CONTENTS

1. EDITOR'S NOTE……………………………………….PAGE 3
2. TEN PRESSING QUESTIONS…………………PAGE 5
3. ROOKIE REPORT……………………………………PAGE 8
4. 2014 SLEEPERS………………………………………PAGE 13
5. 2014 BUSTS……………………………………………PAGE 18
6. POSITION RANKINGS…………………………PAGE 23

Editor's Note

To Our Loyal Readers:

It seems like just yesterday that yours truly was writing out the Editor's Note for the 2013 Fantasy Football Draft Guide as another exciting season was on tap. Just a few months later we saw Peyton Manning put up the greatest offensive season ever in fantasy football, Nick Foles emerge as the biggest breakout passer in the game, and the running back position take another hit downward in the evolution of the passing era. As the 2014 season beckons, it is beyond obvious how the game of fantasy football has changed dramatically from just a decade ago. Gone are the days where running backs dominated the first two rounds of the draft. Instead what we have now is an extreme slant toward quarterbacks and the receivers who catch their passes as the most valuable players in today's game with no signs of the trend letting up. It is that theme that we focused very heavily on in the 2014 Fantasy Sports Boss Fantasy Football Draft Guide, which marks our seventh year in the business of helping our readers to league championships and the bounties that go with it. Once again our staff has gone to great lengths to bring you the latest and most in-depth coverage of the game of fantasy football so that all the bases are covered when you sit down for the very crucial draft. While you can't win your league based solely on your draft results, you most certainly can lose it. On these subsequent pages we bring you the annual top rookies, sleepers, and busts; to go along with our offseason report where we take a look at all of the prime players who changed teams via free agency/trades and how it impacts the game of fantasy football. Finally we attack each of the prime fantasy football positions (QB, WR, RB, TE, K, and DEF) with well-thought out rankings and profiles in order to get to the bottom of who should be placed ahead of who on your cheat sheets.

Of course the work doesn't end once the last pick of the draft is made. Thus your next best course of action is to follow along on the Fantasy Sports Boss website (www.thefantasysportsboss) all season long as we bring you daily injury updates, weekly features such as Player Analyzers, ADDS and DROPS, START/SIT, and our position wrapups after each game. We are constantly striving to stay on top of the competition when it comes to presenting the most useful and insightful fantasy football information one can get as our success is solely a result of all of you. As always best of luck for a great season and we will be there with you every step of the way.

Sincerely,

Michael E. Keneski

The Fantasy Sports Boss

www.thefantasysportsboss.com

2014 FANTASY FOOTBALL TEN PRESSING QUESTIONS

By Michael E. Keneski

Each and every fantasy football season brings with it a whole new set of questions and debates that help shape the draft and the outlook of the upcoming year. 2014 is certainly no different on that front and so with that said here are ten of the more prominent questions that we culled from our mailbag which hopefully lends a bit more clarity as drafts beckon.

1. Q: First let's start with the obvious. Is there any way you can argue that Denver Broncos quarterback Peyton Manning is NOT the top pick in standard league formats this season?

A: This is not worth even discussing really. Anyone who throws for 55 touchdowns and 5,477 yards renders moot any discussion that someone else should be selected ahead of him. As if this wasn't already cemented in stone, the only worry anyone ever had with Manning going back to last season was his four-times over surgically repaired neck. However Manning's offseason visit to a neck specialist came back all positive which means there really is no reason for him not to be the top pick in all standard leagues.

2. Who makes up the rest of Round 1 in a standard 12-team league?

A: Once Manning is off the board, he will likely be closely followed by Aaron Rodgers, Drew Brees, Jamaal Charles, LeSean McCoy, and Calvin Johnson. Those six are the consensus top half of round 1. The next six names to complete the round should mostly center on Adrian Peterson, A.J. Green, Demaryuis Thomas, Marshawn Lynch, and Eddie Lacy.

3. Among those projected first round picks, who carries the most risk?

A: Given the annually horrid Green Bay offensive line, Rodgers could get injured again like he did in missing 7 games a year ago. In addition Peterson is getting to the danger zone age for running backs as he is now 29 with a ton of wear on his tires.

4. Moving beyond Round 1, who makes the cut over the next 12 picks in Round 2?

A: In fantasy football it is crucial that you get it right during the first two rounds as any blown pick there sets you up for failure off the bat. So with that said the next 12 names who should be taken off the board are Matt Forte, Montee Ball, Zac Stacy, Doug Martin, Matt Ryan, Jimmy Graham, Dez Bryant, Julio Jones, Brandon Marshall, Antonio Brown, Alshon Jeffery, and Le'Veon Bell.

5. Who get the nod between Rodgers and Brees right behind Peyton Manning?

A: This is one of the toughest calls of the early portion of the draft as both Brees and Rodgers are virtually identical in value and expected numbers. However the fact Brees plays half his games in a dome and Rodgers has a rough offensive line that could lead to injury, the New Orleans QB is the way to go.

6. How about the same question between Jamaal Charles and LeSean McCoy?

A: The two most exciting and explosive players in the NFL are head and shoulders above the rest of the running back class and will be gone in the first four or five picks. Very tough call between the two but we side with McCoy given the fact he has been a bit more durable than Charles in their respective careers and the Eagles offense is as high-flying as it gets.

7. Is Jimmy Graham worth a late first round pick?

A: Graham is the only tight end you can even think about drafting in Round 1 and he really is a wide receiver in a tight end's body as he finished 2013 with a monster total of 16 touchdown grabs and 86 catches for 1,215 yards overall. So based on the numbers, absolutely Graham makes the grade as a late first round selection.

8. What is the deal with Josh Gordon?

A: Other then that he is a complete idiot? Gordon tested positive for drugs again during the offseason which means he will be suspended anywhere from 8-16 games (a ruling had yet to come down as of this writing). That means a guy who was in the running to be the second receiver off the board after Calvin Johnson is now nothing but a late round pick if he somehow avoids a season-long suspension. Just a complete joke as Gordon was due for a hefty payday after this season as a free agent if he could have just stayed on the straight and narrow.

9. Demaryuis Thomas, Dez Bryant, or A.J. Green after Megatron goes off the board?

A: Very tough call among these three but we will once again go back to the well and say Green is the guy who deserves the number 2 receiver designation. Bryant is too volatile and has had injury issues the last two seasons so he is the quick out in this discussion. Thomas is right there with Green but we went with the latter due to the fact he has less competition for catches.

10. PPR or standard?

A: PPR all the way. If you want the more realistic setup for your fantasy football leagues, than PPR is the way to go. Standard leagues are way too dependent on touchdowns which means goal-line backs could actually have more value than someone with a bunch more rushing yardage. In addition PPR formats deepen the pool of impact players which makes leagues more competitive, as guys like Darren Sproles, Pierre Thomas, Julian Edelman, Wes Welker, and Jason Witten carry more value than in standard formats.

There you have it. As always we welcome questions all season long at The Fantasy Sports Boss where you can e-mail us directly with your queries.

2014 ROOKIE REPORT

By Eric C. Wright

Once again the 2014 NFL Draft was a smashing success, hammering NHL and NBA playoff games in television ratings as fans of all 32 teams tuned in to watch who would be joining their respective organizations. The NFL Draft is also the perfect time to start analyzing rookie passers, runners, and receivers with an eye on the upcoming fantasy football season. While most of these players will either ride the bench or struggle in the early going as they adjust to life in the NFL, some will explode out of the gates and supply top end fantasy football production as we see every year, In addition it is not only the first round guys who supply this instant burst. Late round gems such as sixth rounder Alfred Morris in 2012 have instantly become fantasy football assets when no one even heard of their names going into Week 1. So with all this in mind here are some of the prime names to know going into the new season and what their possible impact could be from the angle of fantasy football.

QUARTERBACKS

1. Blake Bortles: The first passer selected in the 2014 draft was a surprise to many as the Jaguars seemed certain to grab Johnny Manziel in order to inject some life into a moribund franchise. However the Jags cast their lot with Central Florida's Bortles who is expected to back up veteran Chad Henne for a few weeks as he gets up to speed with the offense. Bortles reminds many of Ben Roethlisberger with his size, good arm, and ability to evade the rush to buy more time in the pocket. However his upside is very limited this season given the utter lack of offensive talent at his disposal. Not to be drafted.

2. Derek Carr: The rocket-armed Fresno State product enters into a chaotic situation with the Oakland Raiders who haven't contended in years and whose front office has been a huge mess. However Carr will get to learn for maybe a full season behind veteran Matt Schaub and like with Bortles in Jacksonville, the lack of talent on the Raiders offense make a draft investment here a poor decision.

3. Johnny Manziel: Despite the Cleveland front office already coming out and saying Brian Hoyer will begin the year as the starter, Manziel figures to get drafted in almost all formats, so big is his name brand already. The Browns had a nice thing going with Hoyer as the starter last season so he deserves another look and Manziel himself said he has to earn the job. There are a ton of question marks about Manziel's ability to adapt his game to the size and speed of the NFL but there is no doubting his knack for making plays out of nothing. Again the name itself will ensure Manziel is drafted in all formats and he has as good a chance as Bortles to play early on. However there will be a steep learning curve here which means Manziel is going to be a guy whose best value comes as a trade chip since someone will want to own "Johnny Football."

4. Teddy Bridgewater: Those who purchased our 2014 NFL Draft Guide will know that we had Bridgewater as the top rated passer among all eligible players and we stand by that assessment. In addition Bridgewater has the best chance to make a positive fantasy football contribution out of any rookie quarterback due to the fact the Vikings have already stated he could start Week 1. Despite the pitfalls that inhibit all rookie passers, there is no doubting that Bridgewater has a vast stable of weapons to help him out in the form of RB Adrian Peterson, and wide receivers Greg Jennings and Cordarelle Patterson. The Vikings will simplify the offense for Bridgewater early on which will help and Peterson should do his part keeping defenders out of passing lanes. While we are not suggesting Bridgewater will be anything close to a weekly fantasy football starter, all things considered we believe he has the best chance to put up some useful numbers later on in the season.

RUNNINGS BACKS

1. Bishop Sankey: The running back position has been de-emphasized in the NFL Draft but we still see rookies come in each and every season putting up big time fantasy football numbers like Zac Stacy and Eddie Lacy in 2013 and Alfred Morris the year prior. Sankey figures to join that group this season as he will get a big time look from the RB-needy Tennessee Titans. With only mediocre power back Shonn Greene possibly standing in the way, Sankey is in line to replicate what we saw out of Giovani Bernard with the Cincinnati Bengals last season as a possible RB 2. Sankey was one of the best running backs in all of college football in 2013, catching passes out of the backfield whil running a 4.49 40 which speaks to the home run potential. We are confident enough to give Sankey a RB 2 grade right out of the gate based on his tools and prime opportunity to get meaningful carries

2. Carlos Hyde: The San Francisco 49ers drafted Hyde with a possible eye on replacing aging veteran Frank Gore in the near future. While Gore has been pretty durable the last couple of seasons, Hyde has fresh legs and comes off a very good tenure with the Ohio State Buckeyes. There is limited upside here in fantasy football terms though as Hyde doesn't catch the football and is slow of foot with a 4.62 40 time. He looks destined for spot duty and maybe goal-line work which means little with regards to his fantasy football impact.

3. Andre Williams: The Giants made a smart pick when they took the very productive Williams in the fourth round of the draft but the team's backfield is very crowded with Rashad Jennings, Peyton Hillis, and David Wilson. Even if Wilson doesn't get cleared to return to the field, Williams still has two veteran backs ahead of him on the depth chart. Like Carlos Hyde, Williams is a strict straight-ahead runner who can't catch passes. Not interested.

4. Terrance West: The small-school product out of Towson was an interesting pick by the Cleveland Browns who need all the help they can get at running back. The team has vowed to run the football all day long which means West could get a piece of the action behind starter Ben Tate. West was a horrible blocker in college though so he could have a tough time getting on the field.

5. Tre Mason: The Rams have their own version of Darren Sproles after taking the jack-of-all-trades Mason in Round 3 of the draft. While Zac Stacy is the clear starter for the Rams this season after an eye-opening rookie campaign, Mason figures to make his presence felt in the running, receiving, and return game due to the potential of his explosive speed. Outside of Bishop Sankey, we think Mason has the best chance to contribute this season in fantasy football terms but only in PPR formats.

WIDE RECEIVERS

1. Sammy Watkins: The top receiver by a mile in the draft, Watkins ended up in a bad spot with the offensively-challenged Buffalo Bills and their green QB E.J. Manuel. It is still up for major debate regarding whether or not Manuel is much of a passer and that will have a negative trickle down effect on Watkins. In addition the awful weather; with snow and wind dominating in December, make it unlikely Watkins will contribute many impactful plays when his fantasy football owners need him the most in December when league titles are clinched. Worth a bench spot for now.

2. Mike Evans: Now this guy is interesting. Texas A@M's Evans ended up in the far better situation than did Sammy Watkins after being picked by the Tampa Bay Buccaneers. With the Buc's throwing the football more than ever last season, Evans goes into a nice setup where Vincent Jackson on the other side of the field will take defensive attention away from him. Blessed with tremendous size and speed, Evans is likely to outproduce Watkins and thus might be able to sneak in as an every week WR 3.

3. Kelvin Benjamin: With Steve Smith now a Baltimore Raven and Brandon LaFell in New England, there is a golden opportunity at hand for Florida State's Benjamin to step in as a big part of the Carolina Panther passing attack. At the very least Benjamin will be a huge red zone target as he was in college so he has instant credibility as a standard league WR 3.

4. Odell Beckham: The Giants needed more big plays out of their wide receivers and they likely completed that task by drafting this big play LSU star. Beckham will play a ton right away on the outside opposite former Tigers teammate Reuben Randle as Victor Cruz generally lines up in the slot. Beckham could do a Hakeem Nicks 2010 impression with a solid amount of scores and decent reception totals. The Giants will throw the ball a lot this season under the leadership of new pass-happy coordinator Ben McAdoo which means Beckham could be in the discussion as the most productive rookie wideout in the game for 2014.

5. Brandin Cooks: Sleeper alert! Out of every receiver drafted this past May, Cooks has the most immediate upside due to the fact he got selected into a gold mine for passing with the New Orleans Saints. With rickety Marques Colston aging right before our eyes in a rapid way and with Lance Moore skipping town, Cooks could actually start right away and catch 70 balls. This is the guy we would advise picking if you had only one choice among the rookie receiver class.

6. Marquise Lee: The Jaguars have a major need at receiver and pretty much at any other offensive position on the field. With Justin Blackmon a non-factor due to suspension, Lee has a chance to start opposite Cecil

Shorts. Having the perennially awful Chad Henne under center or rookie Blake Bortles and the growing pains he will have to undergo to deal with, Lee is not likely to do much other as a rookie.

7. Jordan Matthews: Chip Kelly was reportedly obsessed with Jordan Matthews going into the season so he obviously has some big plans for the rookie receiver out of Vanderbilt. Related to Jerry Rice, Matthew has the genes down pat. Riley Cooper is locked in on one side of the field and the recovering from a torn ACL Jeremy Maclin is on the other. If Maclin is not up to par or has a setback, Matthews becomes interesting.

TIGHT ENDS

1. Eric Ebron: The top tight end drafted, Ebron was tabbed by the Detroit Lions at number 10. While Jace Amaro might be the slightly better overall receiver, Ebron has the total package as far as his athleticism and contributions to the passing game is concerned. The problem is that Brandon Pettigrew remains as the starter and he has proven himself to be a very solid receiver. In addition there is a certain guy by the name of Calvin Johnson who will dominate the passing numbers. Bench option at best.

2. Austin Seferian-Jenkins: Seferian-Jenkins joins the potential juggernaut in Tampa Bay as a pass-catching tight end which the Buccaneers haven't had in years. Getting clear starter snaps, Seferian-Jenkins could outproduce Eric Ebron given the fact he will be involved more in the offense from the start.

3. Jace Amaro: Amaro surprisingly slipped to the second round where he was tabbed by the New York Jets to serve as a security blanket for second-year passer Geno Smith. Amaro put up crazy receiving numbers last season for A@M and Smith is in desperate need of playmakers so this could be a great match. Amaro at worst is a bench option who could turn out to be starter-worthy if all breaks right.

As always the performances of rookies in fantasy football is a fluid thing and prone to volatility. Don't ever reach too high for a rookie given all the pitfalls for a first-year player but the potential for a nice breakout is always in play. You can continually check in at The Fantasy Sports Boss (www.thefantasysportsboss) for rookie updasleeperentire 2014 season.

2014 FANTASY FOOTBALL DRAFT SLEEPERS

By Jonathan Curry

We all love sleepers. The fantasy football passers, runners, and receivers who are bursting with potential and who could supply some of the biggest bang for the draft buck. Unfortunately the last part of that previous statement sometimes doesn't always ring true as the fierce annual competition for unproven players can get out of control, thus resulting in players getting drafted higher than they should. However there are in fact some very interesting sleeper plays worth knowing at the very least before you go into your draft. While not all of these players will make good on their potential, some will turn out to be the newest fantasy football revelations. Below are the players we think fit those descriptions for the upcoming season (rookies not included):

QUARTERBACKS

Josh McCown: How about the offensive weapons at this guy's disposal? Not only does free agent arrival McCown have an All Pro wideout in Vincent Jackson and one of the better runners in football in Doug Martin at his disposal, the Buccaneers than went out and picked one of the best receivers in the 2014 draft in Mike Evans and then later picked top tight end prospect Austin Seferian-Jenkins. We all saw in McCown's terrific second half run as the Chicago Bears starter in place of an injured Jay Cutler (13 TD/1 INT) that he can be a very solid performer when given the chance. While he may not play as well on a game-to-game basis as he did last season, McCown is capable of being an every week guy given how vast his weapon arsenal is.

Ryan Tannehill: Third-year passer Ryan Tanenhill has the classic look of a kid who is ready to become one of the better quarterbacks in the league. Despite having arguably the worst offensive line in football which constantly forced Tannehill to abandon the pocket, the Miami gunslinger still vastly improved on his 2012 rookie numbers by throwing for 24 touchdowns and 3,913 yards. When you double your TD output from one season to the next, you are doing something right and Tannehill has the look of someone who could even improve some more as he enters into his third season. For the first time in his career Tannehill will have an accomplished running back to help take pressure off him in the form of free agent signee Knowshon Moreno. With his underrated ability to also collect bonus yardage on the ground, Tannehill could make the leap to every week number 1 guy in single-QB formats.

Michael Vick: We are not buying this whole Geno Smith is the starter bit no matter how times it is repeated by the New York Jets front office. Michael Vick is the much more talented passer (and runner) and he could easily take the Jets places that Smith can't given how awful the West Virginia product was in his rookie season a year ago. While Smith is likely to break camp as the starter, it may only be a matter of time before Vick is under center where he would regain fantasy football relevancy.

RUNNING BACKS

Ben Tate: One of the more prominent sleepers in our view, Tate has been given a tremendous opportunity to serve as the bellcow running back for a very needy Cleveland Browns offense. Tate has shown in the past when starting in place of an injured Arian Foster that he is capable of contributing both in the running and receiving game and new Browns head coach Mike Pettine vowed to "run it all day." Tate could break into top ten territory among all runners if he can just avoid the injury bug that has bitten him in the past.

Toby Gerhart: Gerhart finally gets out from the monstrous shadow of Adrian Peterson by taking his power running game down south to Jacksonville. Right along the same lines of Ben Tate, Gerhart showed intriguing ability when given the chance to start for an injured Peterson. Not only was Gerhart a solid runner who was capable of scoring from in close, he also showed soft hands that allowed him to be a help in the passing game. Could put up RB 1 numbers if all goes according to plan.

Andre Brown: We all know Arian Foster is on the way down both performance-wise and physically. All those years of heavy usage have caught up with Foster in a very bad way and more injuries could be in play for 2014 which means Brown could get up off the bench and be the overnight starter. Brown showed the last two seasons with the New York Giants that he can be a very useful across-the-board performer but his own injury history has to be overcome in order for this to work. At the very least all Foster owners need to back him up with Brown during the later stages of the draft.

WIDE RECEIVERS

Reuben Randle: Yeah the drafting of former LSU teammate Odell Beckham could change the narrative here a bit but the New York Giants also use Victor Cruz almost strictly out of the slot so Randle should be able to start every week on the outside. Possessing some big play ability and a nose for the end zone, Randle has instant standard league appeal at the very least.

Jeremy Maclin: Maclin missed all of 2013 after tearing his ACL in camp but he returns fully healthy (at least for the time being) to a Chip Kelly attack that is the talk of the NFL due to its extreme potency. Many in the fantasy football community and even at your draft likely have forgotten about Maclin but he could return in a major way as the starter opposite Riley Cooper. The Eagles need to replace the production lost when they cut loose DeSean Jackson and Maclin is completely capable of doing so.

Emmanuel Sanders: Big time potential here for a significant breakout as Emmanuel Sanders couldn't have found a better home as a free agent this past offseason. Sanders is poised to take over the starting receiver spot left by Eric Decker and the 10 touchdowns that went with it. Basically if you are a Denver Broncos player with a number that starts with "8" on your chest, you have very interesting fantasy football appeal.

Golden Tate: We will try this one more time with Tate who has been a perennial tease since being drafted by the Seattle Seahawks out of Notre Dame. He signed on as a free agent with the Detroit Lions who have a QB in Matthew Stafford much more capable of getting him the football down the field than Russell Wilson could. There could be a very cheap 8-10 touchdowns here.

Tavon Austin: With Sam Bradford missing most of the season with injury, not to mention some rookie struggles, it was a bit of a rough debut for the St. Louis Rams' do-everything Tavon Austin. It was only a year earlier at West Virginia where Austin caught more than 100 passes his last season in Morgantown so the potential is through the roof here if Bradford cooperates. If operated out of the slot on a consistent basis, Austin could be a sweet PPR steal.

Jarrett Boykin: Boykin was a revelation the second half of last season when he jumped off the bench to put up near-WR 2 numbers in place of an injured James Jones. Now with Jones having signed with the Oakland Raiders as a free agent, Boykin will now be the every week third wideout in the high-powered Green Bay passing attack. That means Boykin should be able to replicate Jones' WR 3 numbers from the last few seasons at the very least.

Jerricho Cotchery: The Carolina Panthers are desperate for some WR help after saying goodbye both to Steve Smith and Brandon LaFell. Cotchery and his TD-heavy approach come to town looking to help any way he can. Cotchery has shown he is capable of the big play and he very well could immediately shoot right to the top of the wide receiver hierarchy in Carolina given the dearth of weapons there. Back in his early New York Jet days Cotchery was a very solid WR 3. He should be back in that realm for 2014.

TIGHT ENDS

Dennis Pitta: We will reprise our glowing sleeper endorsement of Baltimore Ravens tight end Dennis Pitta for 2014 after his 2013 season was almost completely ruined by a hip injury. Pitta returned for the last four games of the season however where he caught 20 balls that served as a nice preview of what he could do over a full year. Joe Flacco loves throwing to the tight end and 80 catches is not out of the question here. Be aggressive.

Zach Ertz: Lots of tight end sleepers this season as many young players are stepping up into positions of prominence which is a group Ertz is a part of. Brent Celek is fading quick which means Ertz is in line to be the starting pass catching tight end in the explosive Eagles offense. That opportunity and location alone make Ertz very appealing.

Jordan Reed: A bad concussion finished Reed off early during his rookie year last season but that only means he falls into the "out of sight/out of mind" realm among the fantasy football community. Reed has terrific receiving ability and if he didn't suffer the concussion last season, he could have finished as a top ten guy.

Ladarius Green: Antonio Gates is still in town and actually coming off one of his better seasons so there is a limit to the immediate upside here. However Green reminds me of a young Gates with his freakish athleticism and speed. Gates is no sure thing to stay healthy as we all know and if sidelined, Green could be a monster performer in his place.

Charles Clay: Not enough was mentioned about the great season turned in by the previously unknown Clay last year when he caught 69 passes for 759 yards and 6 touchdowns. Ryan Tannehill was running for his life all last season which made throwing to Clay his only option at times and the two figure to reprise their very successful connection again in 2014. Upward he goes.

As we said earlier, some of these guys will pan out and some will fall flat on their faces. That is the allure and the danger of the fantasy football sleeper each drafting season. In addition you can follow along on all the sleeper news weekly at The Fantasy Sports Boss (www.thefantasysportsboss.com) where we profile all the upstart performers in order to stay on top of the game.

2014 FANTASY FOOTBALL DRAFT BUSTS

The flip side of the fantasy football sleeper is the dreaded bust. The guys we all try to dodge and avoid outright given the chaos and destructive tendencies they bring to a roster. Sometimes they are impossible to avoid such as when injuries strike down a big time player like what we saw from Aaron Rodgers last season. Other times a player can just have an off-year that plummets his numbers and leaves his fantasy football owners looking at a statistical deficit. Either way avoiding draft busts is not an exact science. However we can at least identify some high-risk players who you are probably better off avoiding altogether this season for a number of differing reasons. Below are those such players who we are going to take a pass on in drafts in order to let them be someone else's issue.

QUARTERBACKS

Robert Griffin III: Griffin III makes the bust list for the second season in a row after he made good on that label in a incredibly poor 2013 campaign. Showing none of the zest and pinpoint passing from his rookie year, Griffin crashed back to earth with a thud last season in throwing only 16 touchdowns with 12 interceptions while failing to build on his 3,200 passing yardage. In addition Griffin lost almost half of his rushing yards as well (from 815 to 489) as knee trouble and the Redskins' desire to keep him in the pocket to avoid injuries took their toll on that aspect of his game. The lack of touchdowns is a big red flag when it comes to fantasy football as you want to get at least 25 there from your top passer. In addition Griffin remains one of the bigger injury risks in all of football due to his slight frame and propensity to not go out of bounds when he can while on the run. There is juat way too much volatility to even bother with and the name greatly outpaces the actual production.

RUNNING BACK

Adrian Peterson: Yup we went there. How on earth can we possibly label AP a draft bust after he comes off yet another big time season in 2013 when he rushed for 1,266 yards and 10 scores? Well for one how about this number? 29. That is the age of Peterson in 2014 which is dangerously close to the scary number 30 that is generally accepted as the mark where steep decline begins to set in for a running back. Peterson has been a workhorse back for seven years now with a ton of pounding on his body. As a result Peterson is starting to break down a bit physically as he has missed 6 games over the last four years. There are only so many yards and carries a runner can get before the breakdowns start to occur and as always you want to leave the party a year early instead of a year too late. While Peterson is fully capable of another big time season in 2014 due to the extreme shape he is in, one only has to look at the massive dropoff from Steven Jackson in 2013 as prime evidence that the tires come off eventually for everyone no matter how good they are.

DeMarco Murray: He is doing it again. Murray is gaining a big following for 2014 fantasy football after he performed as a top five runner the second half of 2013 both in the running and receiving game. The 14 games Murray logged a year ago were the most of his three-season career which gives you an idea how injury-prone he has been. We understand completely the allure of Murray, especially in PPR leagues as he is capable of being a top tier running back if he can ever stay completely healthy. However Murray simply is not capable of staying healthy which means he doesn't jive with the goal every fantasy football owner should have regarding the idea of constructing your roster with as little injury risk as possible.

C.J. Spiller/Fred Jackson: This time around we will link last year's bust candidate Spiller with teammate Fred Jackson due to the arrival of Bryce Brown who came over in a draft day trade from Philadelphia. It is now old news that Spiller can't handle being an every down back due to his injury history and his flat out poor running at times. However Jackson now could be in trouble as Brown could sneak in and take away some of his workload also. Brown is a fresh back with upside who could spell trouble for both guys which means investing in the Buffalo backfield altogether is foolish given the uncertainty of who will be the leading runner.

Frank Gore: Simply put it is amazing how Gore continues to defy the pull of his age as he once again churned out a Pro Bowl season in 2013 at 30-years-old. Another year older at 31 means the likelihood of Gore encountering his cliff season is becoming very concerning. The 49ers revealed their concerns as well by drafting highly-regarded Ohio State power back Carlos Hyde in the draft which means they could be thinking that dropoff is coming as well. Gore has been one of the most underrated great backs we have seen in awhile but now is definitely the time to get off the train before it derails.

Maurice Jones-Drew: An interesting phenomenon in fantasy football is when a player changes teams either through free agency or through a trade, he gains some more appeal despite what the numbers are saying. Such is the case in Oakland where longtime Jacksonville Jaguars RB Maurice Jones-Drew was brought in as a free agent to help revitalize their running game. The only problem is that Jones-Drew is already well on his way toward a career decline after averaging only 3.4 yards per carry last season. Jones-Drew has taken a pounding the last couple of seasons on his squatty frame and his days as a top back are long over. The Raiders have major issues on their offensive line and a poor passing attack so things won't be getting any better.

WIDE RECEIVERS

Julio Jones: On talent alone Julio Jones is right up there with any receiver in fantasy football, including Calvin Johnson. However Jones' body doesn't always come along for the ride as he has had scores of injuries going back to his days with Alabama. Last year it was more of the same as Jones was put on IR not even halfway through the season with a broken foot. He is ready to begin 2014 healthy but likely not for long given his career-long health woes. Major bust potential here that is all injury related.

Andre Johnson: Listen we love Andre Johnson as much as anyone as there is no other publication who have praised the guy more than we have. However we have to be honest about Johnson's current situation which is not totally appealing. Despite coming off one of his best seasons ever in a career filled with monster numbers, Johnson now has the sketchy Ryan Fitzpatrick as his quarterback and the additional challenge of staying healthy on 33-year-old legs. Again Johnson is that classic "name guy" who we all feel comfortable drafting but at the same time his age and poor supporting cast make him a guy who stands a good chance of going the wrong way statistically.

Wes Welker: Not only did Wes Welker see his numbers drop on a per game basis when he was on the field during his first season with the Denver Broncos, two concussions in the span of three weeks towards the end of the year highlight the giant red flag that surrounds his name. Another big blow to Welker's head could instantly spell the end of his career and since he operates out of the slot where going over the middle is a prerequisite, this spells trouble.

James Jones: Jones took the money as a free agent and ran to Oakland after a string of effective seasons as the Green Bay Packers' number three wide receiver. However he will soon find the going much tougher in Oakland where wide receivers have often gone to die. Jones will likely not come close to the touchdown and yardage numbers he had while Aaron Rodgers was throwing him passes and he is more likely to be a WR 4 than the WR 3 he will be drafted as.

Stevie Johnson: Not sure why the 49ers made the trade for Steve Johnson during the draft after they already had Michael Crabtree and Anquan Boldin as primary targets for QB Colin Kaepernick. There are not a lot of footballs to go around in the limited 49ers' passing attack so Johnson is going to fall well short of his Buffalo numbers which had him as a solid WR 3 guy.

DeSean Jackson: Our favorite whipping boy is going to be drafted based on his career season a year ago in Chip Kelly's WR-favoring offense but the fact of the matter is that Jackson will see a stark drop across the board in the much more tamped down Washington Redskins passing attack. Cut at least a quarter of last season's numbers away and that is what you will have out of Jackson this year which will surely lead to a ton of frustration for the hotheaded receiver.

TIGHT ENDS

Rob Gronkowski: This one is easy as Gronk is facing his second consecutive season of missed games right off the bat due to the ACL he tore in his knee last December. We hate investing in guys who are already slated to miss games before the season even begins and those who owned Gronkowski a year ago will tell you how frustrating it was having to peruse the injury reports every week wondering if he would play. Don't do that to yourself and instead take advantage of the plethora of prime tight ends sleepers who are available later on.

Antonio Gates: It surely is asking a lot to expect Antonio Gates to stay healthy for a full 16 games like he did a season ago for the San Diego Chargers and his fantasy football owners. Gates has a long and detailed history of leg and foot problems and at 34 it is likely he will once again be dealing with some more issues with his health. In addition Gates is no longer the dynamic threat he was in his younger days so the decline was masked some by the uptick in catches last season. Try not to temp fate again.

Coby Fleener: Many will run back to Fleener after seeing how well he played during his second season in place of the injured Dwayne Allen last season. However Allen is back healthy and ready to pick up where he left off with QB Andrew Luck from 2012 when the two developed a nice rapport. The Colts have a ton of offensive weapons for Luck to throw to so counting on fantasy football numbers from two tight ends on the same team is asking a ton.

We are not saying to avoid all of the players listed above. Instead we are advising caution when entertaining the idea of making an investment here. The issues that these players have are real and concerning but if the price is right then don't hesitate to take advantage if they come with value attached to their names. Just be fully aware of the risks inherent here and guard yourself with backups in case things start going terribly wrong this season.

2014 FANTASY FOOTBALL RANKINGS AND ANALYSIS

QUARTERBACK

Draft Strategy: For the third season in a row, the way to attack the first round of the draft is to look QB first and than everything else second. Never before has the passing game been more potent and record-setting than it currently is and one only has to look at the video game numbers put up by Peyton Manning last season as evidence. We don't have an official stat on this but we would venture that more than half of fantasy football champions in their respective leagues had Manning as their starting QB, so awesome was his level of production. Gone are the days where taking a running back in the first round (and even picking a second back in Round 2) was the slam dunk way to go. Instead taking Manning, Drew Brees, or Aaron Rodgers right at the top is the new recommended play in this era of passing dominance . With the ridiculous numbers these three and others have put up the last few seasons, starting your draft off with a top tier passer sets you up for immediate success, while also serving as a big time tool to overcome some of the shortcomings from the rest of your roster. It is clearly time to forget old habits in Round 1 and embrace the points where they are the most plentiful which is from the guys who are under center.

1. Peyton Manning: Let's get the obvious out of the way which is that Manning or anyone else would be extremely hard-pressed to repeat his beyond belief 2013 production. Tossing 55 touchdowns to go with a ridiculous 5,477 passing yards, Manning was beyond reproach when it came to any player at any position in all of fantasy baseball last season. Thus Manning deserves to be the top pick in all drafts even if you slash 10 scores and 1,000 passing yards from his ledger. Despite losing Eric Decker to free agency, Manning still has quite possibly the best trio of pass catchers in wideouts Demaryuis Thomas and Wes Welker to go along with tight end Julius Thomas. Manning passed the all-important offseason checkup on his surgically repaired neck which eliminates the one possible stumbling block. Cross your fingers and hope you get lucky enough to land the top pick.

PROJECTION: 4,981 yards 48 TD 12 INT

2. Drew Brees: At 35-years-old Brees is aging but is still seemingly at the top of his game as he comes off another superb 2013 season where he threw for 5,162 yards and 39 touchdowns. Brees also was more careful with the football, slashing 7 interceptions from his bottom line total from the year prior. With Sean Payton continuing to make the pass-happy calls, Brees remains one of the surest bets in all of fantasy football. There is little to talk about here as Brees shows no signs of slippage and despite a smallish frame, he has been one of the more durable players in the game.

PROJECTION: 5,018 yards 40 TD 14 INT

3. Aaron Rodgers: For the third time in four seasons, Rodgers missed time with injury and in 2013 that amounted to 7 starts which really put a hurting on his fantasy football owners. We have spoken for years about the sorry state of the Green Bay offensive line and that hasn't changed as we go into 2014. Thus we have to entertain some injury risk when it comes to using your first round pick on Rodgers and it is that threat that has us putting the Green Bay gunslinger behind both Manning and Brees. When it comes to ability and numbers, Rodgers is just as good as anyone in the game. While Rodgers has not approached 5,000 yards like Manning and Brees, he is a good bet for 40 touchdowns and around 4,500 yards if he can get 14 or more starts. Rodgers also is flat in his prime at only 30-years-old so no erosion in his numbers will be seen for quite awhile.

PROJECTION: 4,426 yards 38 TD 8 INT

4. Nick Foles: The new kid on the first round block, Foles was an immediate success in head coach Chip Kelly's potent passing attack for the Philadelphia Eagles in 2013. Reminding many of a younger Aaron Rodgers, Foles carved up opposing defenses from his first start onward which resulted in a staggering 27 touchdowns and a miniscule 2 interceptions in only 13 games. Built very solidly at 6-6 and 243 pounds, Foles has incredible accuracy and poise in the pocket, while also showing the arm to make all the throws. We know Kelly is going to air it out all day long and Foles will be the prime beneficiary of this high-flying attack. Believe in the hype.

PROJECTION: 4,016 yards 35 TD 8 INT

5. Matt Ryan: Long a favorite of the Fantasy Sports Boss staff due to the nice discount he brings to the draft and the big time numbers to stick with the guys mentioned above, Ryan remains entrenched in one of the more explosive passing offenses in all of football with a pair of Pro Bowl wideouts in Roddy White and Julio Jones; not to mention the best third receiver in the game in Harry Douglas. Unfortunately the retirement of Tony Gonzalez is more than a sizable loss as he served as Ryan's main red zone target. Dirk Kotter emphasizes the passing game as much as any offensive coordinator in football so Ryan will continue to be put in position to make plays. Ryan has gone past the 4,500 yard mark in each of the last two seasons and went for 32 and 26 touchdowns in that span as well. A repeat of those numbers puts Ryan squarely into the top five among all fantasy football QB's but at a full round cheaper than the four names listed above.

PROJECTION: 4,561 yards 30 TD 16 INT

6. Tony Romo: If Ryan was 1A in our All Value Fantasy Football Team, Dallas' Tony Romo was 1B. In going with the theme of Romo's career both in real life and fantasy football, you either love the guy or hate him. There is no in between. Romo sees his name omitted from some of the other top fantasy football passers no doubt due to his much-discussed failures to produce in the clutch. A classic example of how real game football issues impact fantasy. However we don't care if Romo doesn't throw a late fourth-quarter TD pass. We only care that he continues to produce scores and yards overall which he has done in top notch fashion each of the last three seasons. Romo's TD output from 2011 through 2013? How about 31, 28, and 31. The yardage? How about 4,184, 4,903, and 3,828. Unfortunately a back injury that led to surgery has his stock a bit cloudy as of this writing but head coach Jason Garrett reported that Romo is ahead of schedule and should be 100 percent ready to go for Week 1. The questions regarding the back will make Romo even more cheaper, thus making him a big time bargain once again. If you wait two or three rounds to grab your QB, this is the guy to take.

PROJECTION: 4,297 yards 28 TD 14 INT

7. Mathew Stafford: Well that didn't end well. After throwing 27 touchdowns with 14 interceptions the first three months of the 2013 season, Stafford proceeded to blow up both his own stats and his owners' chances of winning their league title by throwing only 2 touchdowns with 5 interceptions in December. Reports of a bad attitude and clashes with the coaching staff add to the red flags surrounding Stafford entering the 2014 season. On ability alone, no one has a stronger arm than Stafford but his gunslinging mentality is what gets him into trouble sometimes with the turnovers. With the best receiver in football in Calvin Johnson on one side and free agent signee Golden Tate on the other, Stafford certainly has the weapons to continue to pile up the numbers. There is quite a bit of boom or bust though with Stafford as he also has not been a picture of health in his career. Classic case of loving the arm but not the turnovers. The discounted price is very attractive but this could all go wrong again like it did at the end of last season. Volatile.

PROJECTION: 4,478 yards 27 TD 18 INT

8. Andrew Luck: Prior to last season we said that Luck was ready to join first round territory for 2014. While Luck has not graduated to that lofty tier, there is no denying the extreme ceiling the Colts QB has and that blockbuster season could surely be on tap for 2014. The Colts ran a somewhat conservative offense early on last season which kept Luck's numbers down but by the second half the training wheels were taken off as the team stormed into the postseason. We think Luck will gain back the yardage he lost from 2012 to 2013 and also add about 7 touchdowns to the 23 he tossed during each of his first two seasons. With the returning from injury Reggie Wayne joining budding star T.Y. Hilton and free agent signee Hakeem Nicks, Luck has his best array of pass receiving talent ever. In actuality it wouldn't even shock us if Luck sails well past he 30 TD mark, so great is his potential.

PROJECTION: 4,377 yards 29 TD 10 INT

9. Cam Newton: We can certainly appreciate the diverse set of skills that Newton brings to the fantasy football table as no one combines the passing/running games better than Carolina's fourth-year QB. Newton comes off a 2013 campaign where he threw a career-high 24 touchdowns while becoming more of a passer. The offshoot was a loss of 156 rushing yards and two scores on the ground. We will take that trade off as less running means less chance of injury. However in breaking things down it is easy to see that Newton is clearly a step below the names listed above him in the rankings when it comes to fantasy football quality numbers. A top notch passing season for Newton is 25 touchdowns and 3,750 yards which comes up well short when discussing the top tier quarterbacks. Many like Newton better then we do which is fine but we remain squarely in the realm of having our running backs pick up the rushing yards and our quarterbacks put up the passing numbers.

PROJECTION: 3,831 yards 26 TD 14 INT 575 rushing yards 6 TD

10. Tom Brady: At 37-years-old, Brady no doubt is on the back nine of his career but the Patriots' long-time All Pro remains quite potent. You have to take the dropoff to last season's 25 passing touchdowns and 4,343 yards with a grain of salt as Brady was left with next to nothing in the receiving department after injuries wiped out large stetches of games from Danny Amendola and Rob Gronkowski; plus the whole Aaron Hernandez mess. Brady made do with what he had and still supplied a very solid fantasy football season. Unfortunately the health of Brady's receivers is still a big issue as Amendola can't be counted on to stay on the field and Gronkowski is coming back from a very serious knee injury that could have him out until October. The age doesn't bother us, especially with the way Drew Brees and Peyton Manning continue to perform after reaching 35. Brady remains very durable and is as smart as they come so 25 passing touchdowns should be the bare minimum As long as you don't grade Brady on his 30-plus TD past, you won't be disappointed.

PROJECTION: 4.425 yards 28 TD 10 INT

11. Philip Rivers: In last season's draft guide we recommended a value play on Rivers due to the fact he was unfairly criticized for an off 2012 season after a run of stellar years between 2008-2011. Despite a delivery that makes high school coaches cringe, Rivers was still in the prime of his career and he only suffered a drop in numbers in 2013 due to a severe lack of weapons surrounding him on offense. Rivers however had arguably his best season a year ago in throwing for 32 touchdowns and 4,478 yards. New head coach Mike McCoy and Rivers meshed from the very beginning and with new star wideout Keenan Allen leading way, together reinvenedt the San Diego passing game into a very potent unit. There is no reason Rivers can't repeat his 2013 numbers this season and his still discounted draft price makes him that much more appealing.

PROJECTION: 4.389 yards 29 TD 14 INT

12. Russell Wilson: The encore to Wilson's eye-opening 2012 could not have gone any better as the Seattle Seahawks' QB passed for 26 touchdowns and only 9 interceptions in leading his team to a Super Bowl championship. Winning titles is nice but we are more interested in winning fantasy football championships which is where things could get a bit more complicated when handicapping Wilson's worth. We have no issues with Wilson's ability to make the big play as he has thrown for 26 touchdowns in each of his first two seasons. However with the Seahawks continuing to emphasize the run, Wilson threw for only 3,357 yards which is the lowest total out of the consensus top 12 quarterbacks for this season. To be fair though, Wilson also rushed for 539 yards which helps offset some of the lost passing totals. We like Wilson in fantasy football terms but don't love him when you crunch all the numbers. The 26 passing touchdowns are likely the ceiling of what Wilson can do in the Seattle offense the way it currently is constituted and the loss of Golden Tate is significant. Also even if you combine the rushing and passing yardage, Wilson still comes up short of 4,000 total yards which is a solid negative. You can do better.

PROJECTION: 3,692 yards 27 TD 10 INT, 567 rushing yards/2 TD

13. Ben Roethlisberger: For the first time in five years, Big Ben was able to make all 16 starts for the Steelers which resulted in his most productive season ever with 28 touchdowns and 4,261 yards. Despite their long and proud history of being one of the best running teams in the NFL, the last three years have seen the Steelers transition fully into an offense predicated on the passing attack. A few things to note on Roethlisberger when weighing an investment however. As noted earlier, Roethlisberger has had trouble with injuries during his career due to all the hits he takes behind annually one of the worst offensive lines in football. Also only four times in his 10-year career has Roethlisberger thrown for 20 or more touchdowns (and only once has he reached 30). Finally, Roethlisberger has thrown for 4,000 or more yards only three times but two of those came in the last three years. The injury risk is decent and the Steelers will likely try to balance out the offense a bit more this season with the emerging Le'Veon Bell and free agent signee LeGarrette Blount. Right on the border of 12-team single QB formats.

PROJECTION: 4,201 yards 27 RBI 12 INT

14. Jay Cutler: It was more of the same for Jay Cutler in 2013. Games missed with injury (5 with a severe groin strain), turnovers (12 interceptions in only 11 starts), and some brilliance (19 touchdowns). Despite the rumblings of a QB controversy last season with Josh McCown playing so well in Cutler's place, the Bears didn't bat an eye in letting the former sign on as a free agent with Tampa Bay. The Bears offense remains as explosive as any unit in football, with an All-Pro RB in Matt Forte complementing THE BEST pair or receivers in the NFL in Brandon Marshall and Alshon Jeffery. If Cutler can stay on the field (which has been a career-long challenge as evidenced by missing 13 games to injury the last four years), 25 touchdowns would be a lock. There are red flags aplenty though with Cutler's propensity for getting hurt and turning the football over, not to mention an attitude that is far from exemplary. If it seems like there are a lot of issues surrounding Cutler, that is because there is which makes him somewhat of a headache to invest in. If you want as little chaos as possible on your roster, stay far away from Cutler. If you want some upside guy in a very potent offense, Cutler passes the eye test.

PROJECTION: 3,624 yards 24 TD 16 INT

15. Ryan Tannehill: Ryan Tannehill continued his upward climb during his second year in the league last season by throwing for 24 touchdowns and 3,913 yards on a terrible Dolphins team. Making Tannehill's performance even more impressive was the fact he was able to compile those numbers behind arguably the league's worst offensive line. The Dolphins went right to work patching up the holes on their line during the offseason which can do nothing but help Tannehill take another step forward numbers-wise. Also signing free agent RB Knowshon Moreno was one of the most underrated moves of the offseason as Tannehill will finally get some help on that side of the ball to remove defenders from the secondary. Having the ability to run for 200-plus yards is a nice bonus and Tannehill could move closer to the precious 30-TD mark in 2014 as well. Upwards we go.

PROJECTION: 4,037 yards 26 TD 16 INT 245 rushing yards

16. Colin Kaepernick: We screamed to the rafters in last year's draft guide about how Kaepernick was a bust waiting to happen and overall he lived up to that prediction. Outside of his terrific Week 1 showing against the Green Bay Packers (3 TD's), Kaepernick was shoddy as he barely threw for over 3,000 yards (3,197) and only tossed 21 total scoring passes. The name brand outpaces the actual value that Kaepernick carries which is always a lose-lose proposition in fantasy football parlance. While we love the speed and intangibles Kapernick brings in real-life football, his shaky passing skills and poor decision-making make him a shaky investment as anything more than a backup in single-QB formats.

PROJECTION: 3,429 yards 23 TD 10 INT 504 rushing yards 1 TD

17. Eli Manning: Boy that was ugly. Despite being a two-time Super Bowl MVP and at times very useful fantasy football passer, the New York Giants' Eli Manning was one of the worst performing quarterbacks in the game last season as he tossed an ungodly 27 picks to go with only 18 touchdowns. Making matters worse, the always durable Manning underwent offseason ankle surgery that had him missing the entire allotment of OTA's which is crucial considering the team is installing a new offensive scheme under Ben McAdoo. At 33 Manning is still young but his penchant for turnovers is well established and that is a huge red flag in fantasy football. The new offense figures to have some hiccups early on and the Giants are re-creating the offensive line on the fly, not to mention having to replace Hakeem Nicks at wide receiver. Way too many question marks here to be worth a pick.

PROJECTION: 3,955 yards 26 TD 21 INT

18. Robert Griffin III: Right along the lines of Colin Kaepernick, the Washington Redskins' Robert Griffin III was a guy we advised you all to steer well clear of heading into the 2013 season. His incredibly slight frame and propensity for getting injured are tremendous negatives from a fantasy football perspective and his awful performances last season only added to the negatives. Griffin missed three more games last season with injury and only managed 16 touchdown throws as he clashed with the coaching staff about the direction of the offense. While we admire the very good rookie season Griffin had in 2012, the read option offense was destroyed by opposing defenses a year ago. We are finding very little to recommend here.

PROJECTION: 3,298 yards 18 TD 11 INT 601 rushing yards 2 TD

19. Andy Dalton: Perhaps no other QB this side of Matthew Stafford alternates between brilliant and pathetic more often than Andy Dalton. Transitioning the Bengals offense into a clear passing unit (and a potent one at that), Dalton tossed a career-high 33 touchdowns and 4,293 yards. However Dalton also threw for 20 touchdowns and was horrific in the team's wild card defeat against the Baltimore Ravens. Dalton was not projected to be much of a gunslinger coming out of college but he has been every bit of that since taking the reigns as a rookie. With A.J. Green, Mohamud Sanu, Tyler Eifert, and Jermaine Gresham as big time targets, Dalton should once again be a very good value play considering the fact he will drop in drafts due to his rough finish to 2013. Works best as a QB two in those formats or as a top backup but Dalton has done more than enough to be trusted as a starter in single-passer leagues as well. Just know going in there will be a complete disaster of a start once or twice during the season.

PROJECTION: 4,173 yards 29 TD 19 INT

20. Alex Smith: Smith is the personification of being a better real-life quarterback as opposed to a fantasy football one. Always showing a knack for the clutch play and for winning games, Smith's numbers never jump off the page. 2013 was no different as Smith threw for a good but not great 23 touchdowns and 3,313 yards. One of the best at protecting the football, Smith also threw only 7 interceptions which is a talent not to be overlooked as Jay Cutler/Eli Manning/Matthew Stafford owners can attest. However the Andy Reid-led Kansas City offense's best player is RB Jamaal Charles which means everything goes through him. We love Smith as a QB 2 in those leagues that play use two starters but otherwise he works best as a solid backup who won't hurt you in a pinch.

PROJECTION: 3,425 yards 22 TD 8 INT 321 rushing yards 1 TD

21. Sam Bradford: Four years into his career after being the number 1 overall pick in the 2010 draft, the St. Louis Rams are still waiting for Sam Bradford to have that breakout season many thought would have come already. While Bradford has had some truly horrendous offensive weapons surrounding him since coming into the league, that excuse went out the door last season as rookie Tavon Austin added big play capability to the unit and the breakout of RB Zac Stacy was a godsend to help take pressure off the passing game. To be fair, Bradford threw 14 touchdowns in only 7 games before he missed the rest of the season with a torn ACL, so there were signs that maybe he was in fact on his way toward a special season. Bradford is squarely into QB 2 territory now and the fantasy football community as a whole gives a collective shrug when his name is mentioned. There still remains some upside as Bradford enters into his crucial fifth season so at the very least he should be selected as an interesting backup guy.

PROJECTION: 3,815 yards 23 TD 11 INT

22. E.J. Manuel: Lots of eyebrows were raised when the Buffalo Bills selected E.J. Manuel in the first round of the 2013 draft but his athletic attributes seemed to fit in well enough as the latest read option QB to enter the league. A rib injury curtailed some of Manuel's progress but overall there were some nice signs during his rookie campaign. Manuel's arm can make all the throws and his athleticism allows him to contribute on the ground in the running game. He still is very raw however and the Bills have not been a passing outfit since the days of Jim Kelly which means fantasy football-friendly passing numbers will not likely be part of the equation. In addition there is the matter of the winter weather in Buffalo as the snow and wind makes any QB who plays there an automatic non-starter in the most crucial weeks of the year.

PROJECTION: 3423 yards 18 TD 15 INT 425 rushing yards 2 TD

23. Joe Flacco: After putting together as good a postseason run as any QB in NFL history; culminating in a Super Bowl championship and MVP award, Baltimore's Joe Flacco went right back to his shoddy fantasy football ways with light totals in both the TD and passing yard categories last season. In fact it could be argued that Flacco had his worst season ever in 2013 as he tossed only 19 touchdowns and a career-high 22 interceptions. The Ravens never feature much in the way of an explosive passing offense and that won't change in 2014. You could even do better than Flacco as a backup option.

PRIOJECTION: 3,547 yards 20 TD 16 INT

24. Josh McCown: There is life after 30. The Tampa Bay Buccaneers certainly thought so as they bestowed a two-year free agent contract on a 35-year-old quarterback who was out of the league in 2010 and who has been a career backup. We of course are talking about new Buccaneers starter Josh McCown whose hard to believe 13-to-1 TD/INT ratio while playing in 8 games for the Chicago Bears in place of an injured Jay Cutler convinced new head coach Lovie Smith that he was the guy to lead the team for 2014. This despite the very solid rookie season from the strong-armed Mike Glennon. There is some decent bust potential here as McCown won't have Matt Forte, Alshon Jeffrey, Brandon Marshall, and Martellus Bennett staring back at him when dropping back to throw this season. While Vincent

Jackson no doubt is a number 1 wideout, he tends to run hot and cold and the Tampa Bay running game was horrendous all season even when Doug Martin was healthy. McCown is a classic veteran who has seen it all and will not make the big mistake to hurt his team. However expecting his 8-game run with the Bears to repeat itself over 16 games with the Buccaneers is foolish. No matter how nice the McCown story was last season, he was a career backup for a reason.

PROJECTION: 3,698 yards 23 TD 14 INT

25. Carson Palmer: Palmer continues to forge ahead on the latter part of his career after his first season with the Arizona Cardinals in 2013 was generally considered a success as the team finished 10-6 but missed the playoffs on a tiebreaker. Still Palmer was wild at times and severely up and down like an elevator with his performance as he threw 24 touchdowns and 22 interceptions. The arm is still impressive and Palmer is surrounded by big-time receiving talent in Larry Fitzgerald and emerging star Malcolm Floyd however. A repeat of his 2013 numbers is the safe way to go in projecting from here on out which means leaves Palmer strictly in backup territory.

PROJECTION: 4,172 yards 25 TD 21 INT

26. Matt Schaub: After a generally successful seven-year run with the Houston Texans, Matt Schaub was pretty much run out of town by the fan base after a horrendous 10 TD/14 INT performance in only 10 games for team in 2013. The always QB-needy Oakland Raiders took a shot with the 33-year-old Schaub however and the veteran should at least be able to help the team put up a few more wins in this season. However Schaub has never been a big numbers guy in fantasy football and that trend figures to get worse in Oakland since he no longer has a top five receiver the caliber of Andre Johnson or even a solid running game to help him out. A top season for Schaub now would be around 24 TD's and 3,800 yards which can help during the byes but not as an every week starter in single-QB setups.

PROJECTION: 3,816 yards 23 TD 16 INT

27. Ryan Fitzpatrick: The Harvard alum continues his tour around the NFL as he signed on as a free agent with the Houston Texans after a comeback season in 2013 with the Tennessee Titans. After taking over as the starter in place of the injured Jake Locker, Fitzpatrick proceeded to throw for 2,454 yards and 12 touchdowns in 11 games, while also picking up three rushing scores. Fitzpatrick plays with high energy and he has a prime opportunity with a talented Texans team that has weapons on offense with Andre Johnson, DeAndre Hopkins, and Garrett Graham. Even better the Texans passed on Johnny Manziel with the first overall pick in the draft so this is Fitzpatrick's team for better or for worse. The high interception totals and lack of top end touchdowns throughout his career leave Fitzpatrick strictly in the backup/spot starter tier.

PROJECTION: 3,425 yards 19 TD 15 INT 277 rushing yards 2 TD

28. Geno Smith: Despite the much publicized addition of Michael Vick to be the team's backup, the New York Jets front office and head coach Rex Ryan continue to maintain that Geno Smith is the team's starter for Week 1. Whether you believe it or not, that question won't be answered until training camp or early in the regular season. As far as Smith is concerned, he was one of the worst performing quarterbacks in the league last season as he threw for only 12 touchdowns and a terrible 21 interceptions. Things got so bad that Smith was benched in the middle of a game twice for undrafted rookie Matt Simms. Smith clearly has a long way to go to make inroads both as a firm starter in the NFL and an even longer path to make an impact in fantasy football. Ultimately Vick is the much better player and we think he becomes the starter sooner rather than later. If you draft Geno Smith, you really should be doing something else.

PROJECTION: 3,325 yards 15 TD 19 INT 325 rushing yards

29. Jake Locker: Locker is back for one last chance to claim the starting QB job for the Tennessee Titans after an injury-ravaged 2013 season that had him playing in only 7 games. In between all the injuries, Locker performed decently with 8 touchdowns and 4 interceptions. Accuracy remains a big problem and the injury-prone label is well-worn. In addition Locker is coming back from last season's foot surgery that had him behind in offseason OTA's. Finally, the very good play of backup Ryan Fitzpatrick in Locker's place last season means the latter won't get much of a leash at all if he starts off 2014 in bad form. One of the worst staring passers in the league.

PROJECTION: 3,016 yards 11 TD 10 INT 207 rushing yards 3 TD

THE REST

30. Michael Vick: The best bet among all backups to be useful in fantasy football as Geno Smith has a very short leash. Vick can still be very helpful in spurts as long as he stops acting like a turnover machine and avoids getting hurt.

31. Mike Glennon: Still shocked Tampa Bay ignored all the nice numbers Glennon put up as a rookie last season and instead went with career backup Josh McCown under center. Glennon does have a future.....somewhere.

32. Brian Hoyer: The giant presence of Johnny Manziel overshadows as terrific run by Hoyer last season as the Browns' starter before he went on IR. Hoyer is likely going to move to the bench by midseason for Johnny Football if I were a betting man.

33. Matt Cassel: Despite the drafting of Teddy Bridgewater, the Minnesota Vikings will likely go into the 2014 season with the veteran Cassel as their starter under center. After some solid seasons with the Kansas City Chiefs, Cassel got his walking papers in order to clear room for Alex Smith. Signing on as a backup to the woeful Christian Ponder for 2013, Cassel eventually found himself onto the field for nine games where he threw for 11 touchdowns and 9 interceptions. Not great numbers by any means but Cassel will be trusted to keep the team afloat until Bridgewater is ready. The whole setup is not the greatest recipe for fantasy football success so Cassel should be ignored.

34. Kirk Cousins: We all know RGIII is one hit away from being out so Cousins retains solid enough value. However Cousins was a bit disappointing in his own right in place of Griffin when he played last season.

35. Case Keenum: It looked like Keenum was the latest diamond in the rough quarterback find as the undrafted rookie performed greet early on in place of Matt Schaub last season but than fell on his face under a hail of turnovers.

36. Matt McGloin: Showed decent ability when running out the season for the Raiders a year ago but like with Keenum, way too many turnovers.

37. Chad Henne: Yes he is starting but we can't get behind any Jacksonville Jaguars quarterback, especially a career slug like Henne.

38. Matt Flynn: Green Bay is the only NFL city Flynn is wanted but he has done nice work there in place of an injured or resting Aaron Rodgers during his two stints with the club.

39. Matt Moore: The poor Miami offensive line could have Moore playing at some point. Has nice touch and poise so he could work as a short-term help.

RUNNING BACKS

Draft Strategy: The days of selecting a running back in the first round and than maybe even adding a second one in round 2 are long gone in today's pass-happy NFL. With quarterbacks and receivers putting up record-breaking numbers on a weekly basis, it is imperative to look at these positions first and than come back to the runners a bit later on which would have been unheard of just a few years ago. Evidence of the downgrade of the NFL running back is seen in the real draft itself as gone are the days where a Ki-Jana Carter was the top overall pick or guys like Adrian Peterson, Steven Jackson, and other aging runners were first round selections. In addition with the proliferation of the two-back system in today's game, the depth at running back is as deep as ever which again makes it the smart move to wait on addressing this position. Of course you don't want to get stuck with Trent Richardson and Shonn Greene as your starters but taking your first runner in Round 3 after you get a top wideout and your quarterback sounds about right. There is an endless list of running back 2's in the draft this season so as long as you got a good 1 under your belt, you can choose to wait even longer to secure that type of player.

1. LeSean McCoy: There is LeSean McCoy, Jamaal Charles, and everyone else. Both McCoy and Charles are the most dynamic players in football, so dangerous are both guys in the passing and running game. The arrival of Chip Kelly helped boost McCoy's already top tier numbers to stratospheric heights as he led the NFL in rushing with 1,607 yards and 9 touchdowns. In addition McCoy was once again one of the best receiving backs in football, hauling in 67 balls for another 539 yards and two scores. McCoy's smallish frame has not prevented him from getting a ridiculous amount of work in Kelly's offense and he figures to have another 2-3 years of top play left before decline sets in. While the 90 catches McCoy had in 2010 are an outlier number, there is no argument that the Eagles' All Pro runner is right behind Peyton Manning in the 2014 draft hierarchy.

PROJECTION: 1,479 yards 8 TD/65 receptions 2 TD

2. Jamaal Charles: The arrival of Andy Reid as the new head coach of the Kansas City Chiefs leading into 2014 was just the recipe RB Jamaal Charles needed to elevate himself into a truly elite player. Rushing for 1,287 yards and a career-high 12 touchdowns, Reid used Charles as a workhorse back for the first time in his career and kept him on the field in short-yardage situations which accounted for the boost in scores. In addition Charles was unstoppable catching the football as well, grabbing 70 passes for 697 yards and 7 more touchdowns. In short Charles was a scoring machine and was the best back in all of football when combining hitting paydirt on both sides of the offense. Charles is the very rare player in today's game who can take the ball to the house whenever he get hi hands on it. He stands behind McCoy only due to the fact there have been a few injury issues along the way, with the torn ACL in 2011 standing out. Slight bust potential based on Charles' light frame but overall this is a scoring monster worthy of a top three pick.

PROJECTION: 1,426 yards 11 TD/67 receptions 5 TD

3. Adrian Peterson: The encore to Adrian Peterson's 2,097 yard rushing season in 2012 predictably came up short but the Minnesota Vikings' superstar running back was still pretty good a year ago in rushing for 1,266 yards and 10 touchdowns. Age is now becoming a big focal point with Peterson as he will be 29 this season which is an age when most running backs start to deal with more injuries and erosion in their stats. One of the most physically fit of any player in the league, Peterson no doubt put in the work for another big time year in 2014 if he can stay in the field. The 4.5 yards per carry Peterson put up last season were pretty much in line with his pre-2,000 campaign so no signs of slippage have been seen yet. We are inclined to believe that Peterson will once again deliver stellar numbers across the board for at least one more year before the inevitable fade begins. Not as flashy as the top two guys due to Peterson's lack of receptions but a stud nonetheless even at 29.

PROJECTION: 1,198 yards 10 TD/26 receptions 2 TD

4. Matt Forte: When new Chicago Bears head coach Marc Trestman went on record prior to the start of the 2013 season that Matt Forte would serve as the team's every down back, including red zone carries, the wheels were put in motion for a career year. Forte certainly delivered as he rushed for a career-high 1,339 yards and 9 touchdowns. Michael Bush stayed nailed to the bench when the Bears got near the goal-line and just that one change elevated Forte's stock in fantasy football to its highest level ever. In addition to the boost in rushing yardage and touchdowns, Forte once again proved he is quite possibly the best receiving back in football as he caught 74 balls for 594 yards and 3 more scores. Forte turns 29 this December which is getting up there but he hasn't had nearly the workload that Adrian Peterson has had so the threat of a dropoff is not there yet.

PROJECTION: 1,201 yards 8 TD/68 receptions 2 TD

5. Marshawn Lynch: After looking like his career was spiraling to the abyss with the Buffalo Bills due to off-the-field trouble, Marshawn Lynch found a rebirth in Seattle where for the last three-plus seasons he has turned himself into the best power runner in football. Toting the football over 300 times (not counting the playoffs) each of the last two seasons, Lynch has had a crazy workload as a Seahawk which is a concern as he turns 28. Also in PPR formats Lynch has to be downgraded a bit as he has only topped 35 catches twice in his 7-year career. However Lynch remains the rare bellcow back who is also one of the best touchdown weapons in the game. That should stay in play for another season.

PROJECTION: 1,225 yards 11 TD/ 27 receptions 1 TD

6. Eddie Lacy: The Green Bay Packers hit a home run with their 2013 first round pick as the former Crimson Ride star rushed for 1,178 yards and 11 touchdowns. Despite missing a game with a concussion, Lacy looked like a younger Marshawn Lynch with his ability to run over defenders through the line, while also showing enough wiggle and burst to take it outside. Already one of the best red zone touchdown hawks in the league, Lacy has some receiving ability as well which makes him a top end asset in both standard and PPR leagues. The best is likely yet to come but it will cost a late first round pick to find out. Lacy will be worth it.

PROJECTION: 1,326 yards 12 TD/41 receptions 1 TD

7. Zack Stacy: The best running back waiver wire gem from 2013 was not even a debate as St. Louis Rams rookie 5th round draft pick Zack Stacy was given the starting job at the end of September and than reeled off 973 rushing yards in two-and-a-half months. Another in the Lynch-Lacy mold of power running, Lacy should get close to or surpass the 10 TD mark while also contributing in the passing game. We love the fact Stacy has little competition for carries on an improving Rams offense and he works well in both PPR and standard setups. Upward we go.

PROJECTION: 1,155 yards 10 TD 42 receptions 1 TD

8. Doug Martin: When discussing some of the bigger busts of the 2013 fantasy football season, Tampa Bay's Doug Martin was at or near the top of the list after he played in only 6 games with his stats down across the board before missing the rest of the season with a shoulder injury. Looking nothing like the slam dunk rookie of the year in 2012, Martin averaged only 3.6 yards a carry and scored 1 touchdown in those six games. Even more infuriating was the fact Martin was a non-factor in the passing game as he caught only 12 passes for 66 yards after hauling in 49 just a year earlier. The Tampa Bay line struggled badly last season which was part of the reason for Martin's struggles and the early horrible play of QB Josh Freeman didn't help take any defenders out of the box. With the adequate Josh McCown now under center and with Tampa Bay sporting a ridiculous set of wideouts in Vincent Jackson and rookie Mike Evans to stretch the defense, Martin should find much more open space to operate with this season. In addition McCown likes to throw passes to his running backs so Martin should be able to reclaim his RB 1 status in both standard and PPR leagues. Bank on a nice comeback season and enjoy the discount.

PROJECTION: 1,237 yards 9 TD/45 receptions 1 TD

9. DeMarco Murray: Quite possibly the biggest boom or bust player in the draft, Dallas' DeMarco Murray once again combined terrific production when on the field but also frustrated with his penchant for injuries. In only 14 games Murray did it all to the tune of 1,121 rushing yards and 9 big TD's to go along with a career-high 53 receptions. Murray is potentially PPR gold if he can put in 14 or more games again but there is the rub. So far in three seasons in the NFL, Murray has missed 12 games already with injury so that aspect has to be graded into his draft price. There is little competition for carries in the Dallas backfield so Murray will once again be put in position for monster numbers. We side with rolling the dice, so vast is the upside.

PROJECTION: 1,105 yards 9 TD/51 receptions 1 TD

10. Giovani Bernard: Bernard is our pick as a guy who you can get in Rounds 3 or 4 and who could turn out to be a first rounder by the end of the season. Stunted somewhat as a rookie in sharing time with BenJarvus Green-Ellis, the Bengals began to increase Bernard's workload as the season went on. Bernard rushed for 695 yards on only 170 carries and he made himself a very interesting PPR play as well after grabbing 56 passes for another 514 yards. Possessing explosiveness on par with a LeSean McCoy or a Jamaal Charles, Bernard should get the clear majority of carries this season which will vastly increase his numbers in the rushing department. The only drawback could be the fact the Bengals could continue to give Green-Ellis goal-line work.

PROJECTION: 1,079 yards 7 TD/61 receptions 2 TD

11. Arian Foster: Falling fast. Foster is just the latest example of how a string of very heavy usage eventually leads to the body giving out. From 2010 through the 2012 season, no one was better than Foster as he put up ridiculous rushing and TD totals to go along with big time work in the passing game. Unfortunately all of the pounding that went with all those carries took a toll as Foster started seeing his stats slip in 2012 and then endured a busted season a year ago when a spine issue led to season-ending surgery. Now turning an old 28, Foster is looking on the downside of his career and has to deal with the free agent arrival of Andre Brown to remove him from the workhorse back ranks. It was a fun run while it lasted but just like we saw with Priest Holmes during his short but amazing run at the top with the Kansas City Chiefs, the life of the NFL running back is short. Remember one of the sure ways to lose at fantasy football is so evaluate guys based on past performance or let name brand infiltrate your thinking. Foster is now a declining stock that has major bust potential.

PROJECTION: 1,023 yards 8 TD/38 receptions 1 TD

12. Alfred Morris: While the numbers were down somewhat, Morris did more than enough last season to prove that his eye-opening 2012 rookie year was no fluke. Having posted two straight seasons of more than 1,200 yards rushing and 20 touchdowns his first two years in the league, Morris has now put himself in the conversation as one of the better power runners in the game. Morris is a guy however who sees his value drop sharply in PPR formats as he is a complete non-factor in that aspect of the game, having caught only 11 and 9 passes his first two seasons. While in standard formats Morris fits as a low end RB 1, in PPR leagues he drops sharply to a low end RB 2.

PROJECTION: 1,245 yards 10 TD/10 receptions 0 TD

13. Reggie Bush: Bush looked like he found a home in Detroit last season after inking a sizable free agent contract as he rushed for over 1,000 yards for the second time in his career with 1,006. Always one of the best receiving backs in the game, Bush also chipped in with 54 receptions for 506 yards. However true to his career trends, Bush also left something to be desired as he scored only four touchdowns and missed another game with injury. Only twice in his eight-year career has Bush played in all 16 games and the emerging Joquie Bell is now fully in the picture to take some of the carries and touchdowns away. Bush has much more value in PPR formats where he profiles as a high end RB 2 but in standard leagues he is a low end 2 at best given the lack of touchdowns.

PROJECTION: 987 yards 5 TD/52 receptions 2 TD

14. Le'Veon Bell: Bell was a highly touted rookie sleeper of ours heading into 2013 as the Steelers had a glaring need at running back. The former Michigan State Spartan possessed a very intriguing blend of rushing and receiving skills, making Bell especially attractive in PPR formats. Unfortunately Bell didn't make his debut until late September due to suffering a foot injury in training camp but once back on the field, the results left us all wanting to see more. Bell's running was shaky as he averaged only 3.5 yards per carry but he scored 8 touchdowns in only 13 games, while also catching 45 passes. There is nice ceiling to tap into here as Bell will now have a full training camp under his belt and the lion's share of carries in his future. While Bell should be graded out as a RB 2 going into drafts, he could finish 2014 as a RB 1 given his potential and open path to carries.

PROJECTION: 1,088 yards 10 TD/55 receptions 1 TD

15. Shane Vereen: Vereen is the flip side of Marshawn Lynch when it comes to standard league/PPR values. While Lynch is a monster runner who is light on receptions, Vereen is quite possibly the most accomplished receiver in fantasy football as he operates as Tom Brady's safety valve out of the backfield. Despite playing in only 8 games due to a fractured wrist suffered in the season opener, Vereen caught 47 passes for 427 yards and 3 scores. Extrapolated over a full season, Vereen would have approached 90 receptions which is extremely good in PPR formats. Unfortunately Vereen is a one-trick pony as he ran for only 208 yards. Vereen has a clear role in the Patriots' offense and he does it very well. He is a RB 2 all the way in

PPR formats but nothing more than a 3 in standard leagues given the utter lack of yards on the ground.

PROJECTION: 501 yards 2 TD/72 receptions 5 TD

16. C.J. Spiller: Few players engender as much frustration and annoyance from their fantasy football owners than does Buffalo's C.J. Spiller. If anyone read last years' draft guide, you would have seen we had Spiller down as a decent-sized bust candidate due to his inflated first round draft price. Spiller should never have been a first round pick due to his injury-prone ways and the presence of veteran Fred Jackson who remains a very accomplished runner in his own right and who handles goal-line work. Overall Spiller lived up to the bust hype as he failed to break 1,000 yards rushing (933) and scored only 2 touchdowns on the ground. Even Spiller's skills at catching the football were underwhelming as he caught only 33 passes which left the speedster as a disappointment all the way around. There is no doubting Spiller's game-breaking ability and potential for scoring every time he touches the football. However with Jackson still around to steal carries and Spiller remaining a prime injury risk, downgrading him to a RB 2 is the right call.

PROJECTION: 1,026 yards 5 TD/48 receptions 4 TD

17. Frank Gore: We feel like we have written the same thing about Gore the last three seasons. Getting older but still very productive. The same theme was in play last season as Gore once again made the Pro Bowl in rushing for 1,128 yards and 9 touchdowns. Now 31-years-old, which is ancient for a running back, the cliff season could come at a moment's notice which even San Francisco seems to realize after drafting Ohio State's Carlos Hyde in the second round of this past year's draft. In looking deeper into the numbers last season, Gore's yards-per-carry was down to 4.1 from 2012's 4.7. That 4.1 mark was also the lowest of Gore's career so we could be seeing decline underneath everything already. Also while Gore used to be one of the best receiving backs in football, he has virtually been removed from the offense on that front since Jim Harbaugh came to town. I hate investing in any runner over the age of 30, especially one with so much mileage as Gore has since he has been a workhorse guy every year of his career since being drafted. Salute the great and very underrated career and move on for good.

PROJECTION: 1,092 yards 7 TD/21 receptions 0 TD

18. Ray Rice: Not only did Ray Rice have a terrible year in 2013, he proved in the offseason that he was a terrible guy as well after he was caught on camera physically assaulting his wife. Legal troubles aside, Rice has crashed hard when it comes to his fantasy football value to say the least. For a guy who only two years ago was in the discussion for being the top pick in the entire game, Rice is now barely a RB 2 as it already looks like he is on the decline after only six seasons. Rice rushed for a pathetic 660 yards on 3.1 yards per carry and four touchdowns a year ago. While he still was terrific in the passing game with 58 catches, Rice was benched at times for backup Bernard Pierce. At only 27, Rice is still young but six seasons of taking punishment on his slight 5-8/212 pound frame has caused him to lose a step. Away from the numbers, we don't want a guy who is a wife beater on our teams anyway.

PROJECTION: 901 yards 5 TD/55 receptions 378 yards 1 TD

19. Knowshon Moreno: After finally figuring out how to stay healthy for a full season, Knowshon Moreno blew his numbers out of the park in capitalizing on a free agent year in rushing for 1,038 yards and 10 touchdowns while also catching 60 passes. The talent was never in question for Moreno, as his biggest issue was his penchant for getting injured which caused him to miss 20 games the previous three seasons. While always possessing extreme PPR sleeper value and with Peyton Manning having a season for the ages in the passing game, gaping holes opened up for Moreno to breeze through as he ran all the way to a mammoth contract with the Miami Dolphins to be their lead runner. Moreno will see more defenders in the box with the Dolphins in going from Manning to Ryan Tannehill under center and the team's offensive line has been rough for years. However as long as the health cooperates, Moreno is right on the doorstep of being a RB 1 in PPR formats and a RB 2 in standard leagues.

PROJECTION: 1,099 yards 9 TD/62 receptions 589 yards 1 TD

20. Ryan Matthews: San Diego's Ryan Matthews was in the same boat as Reggie Bush and Knowshon Moreno as talented runners who just could not ever stay completely healthy which led to plenty of angst along the way for their respective owners. However like with Moreno last season, Matthews finally stayed on the field for a full 16-game campaign and the results were his best year ever in rushing for 1,255 yards and 6 touchdowns while also catching 26 passes. Despite the big year there are a few red flags to discuss. The first is that we don't ever advise paying for a career year and banking on a second straight full season out of Matthews would be foolhardy. In addition, Donald Brown signed on as a free agent and he is capable of taking hold of some of the carries at Matthews' expense. Finally, while a very good receiver out of the backfield, Matthews was pretty much taken out of that role in favor of Danny Woodhead who put up a monster PPR year in catching 76 passes. Combined all together, Matthews is a risky RB 2 pick in all formats and one we will cash in our chips on as his value can't go anywhere but down this season.

PROJECTION: 1,010 yards 5 TD/32 receptions 1 TD

21. Danny Woodhead: Right along the lines of Shane Vereen in New England, San Diego's Danny Woodhead is a clear pass receiving running back who is only to be used in PPR formats. Perfecting the route out of the backfield, Woodhead caught 76 passes for 605 yards last season to go with six touchdowns. Woodhead only got 106 carries for 429 yards however which speaks to his limitations. Nothing more really needs to be said here as the numbers speak for themselves.

PROJECTION: 467 yards 2 TD/68 receptions 5 TD

22. Andre Ellington: It was a very nice rookie season for Arizona Cardinals running back Andre Ellington in 2013 as the speedster averaged 5.5 yards per carry while picking up 652 yards on the ground in part-time duty. As the season went on, head coach Bruce Arians got Ellington more involved in the offense as Rashard Mendenhall proved he was not the answer at running back. Showing good versatility, Ellington also caught 39 passes out of the backfield and his top end speed made him a threat to score from anywhere on the field. It would appear Ellington is set for a major uptick in production this season with Mendenhall gone. However Arians has spoken many times about his desire to not overexpose Ellington who stands only 5-9 and 199 pounds. Fearing injury if Ellington carries the ball too much, it looks like Arians wants to sprinkle in Stepfan Taylor to keep both guys fresh. There is still quite a bit of mystery concerning Ellington regarding whether he can hold up physically to the higher workload and what kind of carry allotment he will receive which makes pricing him difficult. In PPR leagues bump Ellington up a bit but in standard formats he could drop down to the RB 3 level as the thicker Taylor could get goal-line work.

PROJECTION: 1,035 yards 5 TD 44 receptions 1 TD

23. Steven Jackson: Stick a fork in him. The Atlanta Falcons gambled that Steven Jackson had something left in the tank prior to 2013 by signing the long-time Ram to a free agent deal and the results were disastrous. The former workhorse stud missed four games with injury and saw his yards per carry average drop way down to a pathetic 3.5. All together Jackson ran for a career-low 543 yards and by the end of the season was ceding carries to Jacquizz Rodgers. The Falcons talked up his health in offseason workouts but they also promptly went out and drafted Devonta Freeman in the third round of the draft. The backfield looks very crowded right now and Jackson could be left behind. Terrific career but you are best left ignoring Jackson completely.

PROJECTION: 817 yards 5 TD/39 receptions 0 TD

23. Maurice Jones-Drew: Father Time spares no one and he certainly went to work on Maurice Jones-Drew in 2013 to say the least. After eight years as the main offensive weapon with the Jacksonville Jaguars, all those carries on a compact 5-7 frame took its toll on Jones-Drew's numbers last season. Showing a very slow first step for the first time in his career, Jones-Drew averaged a terrible 3.4 yards per carry while rushing for only 803 yards in 15 games. Clearly Jones-Drew's days as a workhorse back are over and you can even say the same about his previous status as a RB 1. Still possessing the ability to catch the football (43 catches last season), Jones-Drew passes the test barely as a RB 2 in PPR formats. Again you don't want to invest in a player whose best days are behind them no matter how large the name is.

PROJECTION: 917 yards 6 TD/47 receptions 335 yards 1 TD

24. Darren McFadden: McFadden is back with the Raiders after taking a low ball offer in free agency coming off a horrific 2013 season when he rushed for only 379 yards with a 3.3 per carry average. Injuries once again were the dominant theme as McFadden missed 6 more games, bringing the total there to 29 for his six-year career. In the past we were sometimes willing to look past the injury risk with McFadden due to the fact he was an electrifying runner and receiver but he was downright rotten when on the field last season, minimizing the little appeal he had left. Forget being drawn into this trap again. Also McFadden now has to deal with the free agent arrival of Maurice Jones-Drew to take a good chunk of his carries. McFadden is as sure a bet to get hurt as any player in football and thus should have a big red "X" scribbled through his name on your cheat sheet.

PROJECTION: 517 yards 4 TD/27 receptions 1 TD

25. Rashad Jennings: Who knew Jennings had that in him? After three nondescript seasons backing up Maurice Jones-Drew in Jacksonville and failing to do much of anything, Jennings took advantage of another Darren McFadden injury to put up running back 1 numbers the second half of 2013. Jennings was spectacular at times on both sides of the offense, rushing for 733 yards and 6 touchdowns while averaging 4.5 yards per carry. Even more impressive perhaps were the 36 catches in only 8 starts. Signed to a free agent deal by the New York Giants to replace Andre Brown, Jennings has the inside track to the majority of carries in the team's backfield despite the return of David Wilson and the drafting of Andre Williams. The fact that Peyton Hillis is still on the roster is a concern for the workload of Jennings but at least in PPR leagues he checks out as a RB 2.

PROJECTION: 1,036 yards 7 TD/48 receptions 345 yards 1 TD

26. Toby Gerhart: Sleeper alert! Finally away from the shadow of Adrian Peterson, Toby Gerhart gets his long-awaited chance to start with the RB-needy Jacksonville Jaguars. No doubt facing a tough go replacing longtime star Maurice Jones-Drew, Gerhart showed very good ability in spurts when filling-in for an injured Peterson during his Vikings tenure. Gerhart has averaged 4.7 yards per carry during his four years with Minnesota, where he also showed the ability to be a PPR weapon with soft hands out of the backfield. With the Jaguars having an utter lack of offensive talent, they figure to ride Gerhart all game long which means potentially significant numbers. We recommend a strong play here on Gerhart as the stars are aligned for a breakout season.

PROJECTION: 1,152 yards 9 TD 37 receptions 245 yards 1 TD

27. David Wilson: There were few backflips done by Giants running back and former first round pick David Wilson in 2013 as a bout of spinal stenosis that led to neck surgery finished him off after only 5 games and 146 rushing yards. Flat out Wilson was a colossal bust even before the injury, averaging only 2.7 yards per carry and catching two measly passes. Wilson has been cleared to return to the Giants this season but the team has seemingly moved on from him after signing free agent Rashad Jennings and drafting Boston College Heisman finalist Andre Williams. Don't draft Wilson given the crowded backfield and persistent injury issues.

PROJECTION: 326 yards 1 TD/19 receptions 102 yards 1 TD

28. Chris Johnson: Running for 2,000 yards in a season can only buy you so much time with a franchise as shown by the Tennessee Titans cutting loose Chris Johnson just 4 years after he reached that milestone total. It was from that 2009 season onward that Johnson started to look like he lost a step or two, culminating in a career-low 3.9 yards per carry in 2013 that helped usher in the release. In actuality many were a bit too harsh on Johnson since his 2,000 yard season as he has missed only one start in his career and has had two 1,200-yard plus campaigns in the last four years. In addition Johnson has consistently been one of the better receiving backs in football, having only once failed to grab at least 40 balls in a season. The New York Jets were all too happy to bring him aboard as a free agent but the situation is a bit complicated due to the presence of power back Chris Ivory who figures to get goal-line work. Johnson has indicated his unwillingness to be in a time-share in the past so this needs to be watched. However unlike Johnson, Ivory has a tough time staying healthy so the lion's share of carries could still go his way. Given all we have seen and for the fact Johnson is aging, projecting him as a RB 2 in all leagues is the safe bet.

PROJECTION: 1,097 yards 5 TD/46 receptions 362 yards 2 TD

29. Ben Tate: While Chris Johnson and Rashad Jennings signing with teams that have competition for carries at running back, Ben Tate went to a potential workload gold mine by inking a deal with the Cleveland Browns who have been in dire need of an impact runner for years. Tate has virtually no competition for carries in the Cleveland backfield and new head coach Mike Pettine has said the team will "run all day." That is music to Tate's potential fantasy football owners' ears. Tate has done a nice job in three years backing up Arian Foster in Houston, averaging 4.3 yards a carry or more during that time span to go with solid receiving skills. There is the potential for significant numbers here given the opportunity at hand and so Tate qualifies as a nice value pick with vast upside in both standard and PPR formats.

PROJECTION: 1,126 yards 8 TD/41 receptions 298 yards 1 TD

30. Fred Jackson: Fred Jackson is like a gnat that C.J. Spiller can't swat away. The veteran PPR weapon once again caddied for Spiller in the Buffalo backfield last season and in the end vastly outproduced his teammate. Perenially one of the more underrated runners in the game, Jackson averaged a nice 4.3 YPC in picking up 890 yards on barely over 200 carries. In addition Jackson proved once again that he has sneaky good value in PPR formats after catching a career-high 47 passes for 387 yards. With Spiller a constant health risk and his performance not up to par last season either, Jackson could be in line for another value season. However the late trade for Bryce Brown during the draft is a potential problem as the former Eagle is much cheaper than the veteran Jackson so there is some risk the latter could be a salary-cap cut. Keep a closer eye on how this shakes out before you draft.

PROJECTION: 815 yards 5 TD/35 receptions 238 yards 1 TD

31. Montee Ball: The Denver Broncos cleared the decsk in the offseason for second-year back Montee Ball, choosing not to re-sign starting runner Knowshon Moreno. That leaves Ball in the workhorse role for the Broncos and based on what we saw in his solid rookie season, the former Wisconsin Badger should be up to the task. Despite getting only 120 carries in deference to Moreno, Ball averaged a splendid 4.7 yards per carry and by the end of the season was the goal-line back. Ball was incredibly productive in college and should be able to pick right up where Moreno left off in the running game. However he is not nearly the receiver Moreno was so in PPR leagues Ball should be downgraded a bit. The potential of workhorse carries though puts Ball possibly in the RB 1 class in standard formats and a solid RB 2 in PPR setups.

PROJECTION: 1,032 yards 8 TD/29 receptions 0 TD

32. Darren Sproles: Eagles head coach Chip Kelly has a shiny new toy to play with after pulling off a trade with the New Orleans Saints to acquire do-everything back Darren Sproles. The trade doesn't change Sproles' fantasy football outlook much though as both the Saints and Eagles are right at the top of the league in passing yardage and offensive potency. Sproles has made a career out of being a PPR gem and catching the football will once again be his calling card as he has caught 70 or more passes each of the last three seasons. In actuality Sproles is a wide receiver with RB eligibility. Rate as a RB 3 in standard and a high end 2 in PPR.

PROJECTION: 275 yards 2 TD/ 75 receptions 687 yards 6 TD

33. Pierre Thomas: Few probably realize that the oft-injured Pierre Thomas led all running backs in receptions last season with 77 for 513 yards and 3 scores. While Darren Sproles was right in the ballpark with those numbers, what separated the two was the fact that Thomas is also capable running the football as he has averaged 4.6 yards per carry in his career. This season will be an interesting one for Thomas who has a golden opportunity for his best year ever with Sproles now in Philadelphia and the woeful Mark Ingram posing little threat to his workload. Thomas just has to stay healthy, which has been a challenge in the past, in order to realize his potential. While Sproles is strictly a PPR weapon, Thomas can be a solid RB 2 in standard leagues given his ability to contribute on the ground. A possible career year could be on tap.

PROJECTION: 787 yards 5 TD/65 receptions 498 yards 3 TD

34. Stevan Ridley: It is anyone's guess what Bill Belichick will do with favorite whipping boy Ridley in 2014 after he slammed the door shut on him in the doghouse for a good chunk of last season due to fumbling issues. However Ridley was back in the rotation during the second half of the season and responded well by finishing up with 7 touchdowns on the ground. However Ridley went from 1,263 yards in 2012 to only 773 a year ago so he clearly went down as one of the biggest busts of the season. There is a ton of risk investing here as Ridley's fumbling problems could rear its ugly head at a moment's notice and he doesn't catch passes which lessens the margin for error. We would advise looking elsewhere as you want to invest in as little risk as possible.

PROJECTION: 1,032 yards 8 TD/ 14 receptions 21 yards 0 TD

35. Trent Richardson: I guess the Browns knew something the Colts didn't when it came to RB Trent Richardson last season. Many scratched their heads when the Browns traded Richardson to Indy right at the outset of the 2013 season for a first round pick to after they originally made him the 3rd overall pick in the draft just a year earlier. The Browns clearly got the last laugh though as Richardson was quite possibly the worst performing starting running back in the NFL from that point forward, averaging only 2.9 yards per carry and collecting all of 3 touchdowns in 14 games. Horrific to say the least. No doubt the Colts want to get something out of the deal so Richardson is back as the starter entering 2014 but his leash figures to be much shorter. In truth there were red flags with Richardson even in his rookie year with Cleveland as he averaged only 3.6 yards per carry while seemingly always dealing with some sort of malady. Richardson's injury-prone label is well earned going back to his days with Alabama and the interesting Vic Ballard is ready to take over if all goes wrong again. This is just a speculative situation at this point as Richardson can't be graded as anything more than a bench backup runner.

PROJECTION: 814 yards 5 TD/37 receptions 1 TD

34. Lamar Miller: Miller has pretty much gone bust for Miami since they selected him in the fourth round of the 2012 draft. Knowshon Moreno was signed to be the team's main ballcarrier so Miller is not interesting unless injuries put him in the starting role.

35. Jonathan Stewart: You know you have problems when you best runner is your starting quarterback. That has been the situation with the Carolina Panthers the last three seasons as Jonathan Stewart, DeAngelo Williams, and Mike Tolbert have all failed to put up impact numbers. Stewart himself has seen his once-promising career fall off the rails due to injury as he has missed 17 games the last two seasons. With Williams likely getting the starting nod for what its worth, Stewart is really now nothing more than a RB 4.

36. Joique Bell: The undrafted second-year runner out of gridiron power Wayne State was actually the most productive player in the Detroit backfield last season, which of course included Reggie Bush. Bell was dynamic off the bench for the Lions, excelling both in the running and passing game. Altogether Bell rushed for 8 touchdowns and caught 53 passes in part-time duty which put him in RB 2 status in PPR formats. While Bush is still technically the starter, we all know about his lengthy injury history and the Lions showed how much they value Bell by inking him to a three-year extension during the offseason so he will get his share of work out of the backfield. We like the price as many owners will let Bell slide by due to the presence of Bush but in PPR formats at least, he can surely be a RB 2 help.

PROJECTION: 598 yards 7 TD/55 receptions 587 yards 2 TD

37. Shonn Greene: After Chris Johnson was cut loose by the Tennessee Titans, it appeared as though veteran Shonn Greene would get a second chance at a starting running back job like he had at one time in a failed tenure with the New York Jets. Just when Greene started feeling good about his chances for a big season, the Titans went out and made Bishop Sankey the top running back selected in the draft. Sankey is expected to be the speed portion of a platoon with Greene, thus limiting the latter's potential impact to a bench play at best since he can't catch the football. Greene should be in line for all of the goal-line work but that is the length of his probably impact this season.

PROJECTION: 598 yards 6 TD/8 receptions 15 yards 0 TD

37. Bernard Pierce: Going into the 2013 fantasy football season, Bernard Pierce was a popular sleeper name on many lists. After all with Ray Rice coming off a somewhat disappointing 2012 and Pierce showing nice ability as a rookie, the opportunity was there for a breakout from the second-year back out of Temple. However as bad as Rice was last season, Pierce was maybe even worse as he averaged only 2.9 yards per carry and failed to show any reason for John Harbaugh to play him over his veteran counterpart. Pierce also may not be ready for the start of camp after offseason surgery on his shoulder which further complicates matters. Rice looks shot but Pierce has to earn back some cred before we look here again.

38. Andre Brown: When his health has cooperated, which has been very rare in his short career, Andre Brown has opened eyes with some terrific power running from 2012-13 with the New York Giants. Brown scored 11 touchdowns in only 18 games with the Giants, while also contributing out of the backfield as a receiver. This is not a star by any means and a major breakout is not expected since Brown will cede the starting allotment of carries to Arian Foster. However Foster's health has been just as dicey as Brown's which means the latter could be in the starter role before too long. A must own handcuff for all Foster owners at the very least and worth a bench stash in deeper formats.

40. DeAngelo Williams: Hard to believe that for a brief time in his career, DeAngelo Williams was considered a first round fantasy football talent. Those days are long gone now as Williams is just another mediocre name that can be used to fill out a bench. His quickness has faded and Williams can't stay on the field for an entire season. Move on.

41. Chris Ivory: Ivory will be the thunder to Chris Johnson's lightning this season in the New York Jets backfield. Despite a long history of leg injuries, Ivory stayed on the field for 15 games last season and was far and away the most effective runner for the Jets as he averaged 4.6 yards per carry and 833 yards on the ground total. Ivory is a pure power back all the way who also has some deceptive speed when in the clear. He doesn't add anything in the PPR realm though and the arrival of Johnson shot down some initial excitement about what Ivory could do as the clear starter this season. Bench option in all formats.

PROJECTION: 702 yards 6 TD/4 receptions 5 yards 0 TD

42. Jacquizz Rodgers: Filling the Darren Sproles role for the Atlanta Falcons the last two years, Rodgers has caught more than 50 passes in both 2012 and 2013 and he figures to be the outlet guy once again this season. Rodgers really only has value in PPR formats as Steven Jackson and rookie Dalton Freeman figure to do the majority of running.

43. Khiry Robinson: The undrafted second-year man out of West Texas A@M will now firmly enter into the New Orleans running back committee with Pierre Thomas and Mark Ingram. There is some nice speed potential here but Robinson is not of interest unless something happens to Thomas.

44. Ahmad Bradshaw: Once a firm RB 2 in all formats, Ahmad Bradshaw is heading close to irrelevancy due to his oft-injured feet. Bradshaw got into only three games with the Indianapolis Colts last season and now has to deal with Trent Richardson dominating carries. Nothing happening here worth talking about.

45. James Starks: Starks is the clear backup to Eddie Lacy but he is worth a handcuff in deeper formats due to his ability to help on both sides of the football.

THE REST

44. Donald Brown: Brown never really panned out with the Indianapolis Colts and instead now signs on in a crowded San Diego Chargers backfield. Only has value if something happens to Ryan Matthews which we all know is very likely.

45. Bryce Brown: It didn't get a lot of attention but the Bills swinging a trade during the NFL Draft to net Bryce Brown from the Philadelphia Eagles was interesting since the team already has C.J. Spiller and Fred Jackson. Brown showed some LeSean McCoy-lite ability when he got on the field for the Eagles, running well and catching the football. Fumbles are a big problem but Brown's arrival could mean the end of Jackson's tenure in Buffalo.

46. Mark Ingram: Ingram has not come close to his Heisman hype coming out of Alabama. He is nothing but a straight line runner who can't catch the football and Pierre Thomas is the clear starter.

47. Roy Helu: Helu has a very good and durable back in Alfred Morris ahead of him on the Redskins' depth chart so his upside is extremely limited despite some nice PPR potential.

48. Vic Ballard: The Colts will force feed Trent Richardson this season after stupidly giving up that first round pick to the Cleveland Browns to acquire him early last season which means Ballard is not going to be much of a factor unless injury strikes.

49. BenJarvus Green-Ellis: The Bengals will continue to phase in Giovani Bernard more at the expense of aging veteran Green-Ellis. The Law Firm remains factor near the goal-line however.

50. LeGarrett Blount: The Steelers brought Blount in after the veteran revived his career with the Patriots last season. Blunt is a straight-line power back only as he has little receiving ability. Could hurt Le'Veon Bell a bit if he gets goal-line work which bears watching.

WIDE RECEIVERS

Draft Strategy: Echoing what we have said about the era of the passing game in today's NFL, getting a top number 1 receiver onto your fantasy football roster in the first two rounds is absolutely imperative. With some nice QB values that you can pick up later on in drafts such as Philip Rivers, Tony Romo, and Ben Roethlisberger, it is not the worst idea to take a receiver with your first two picks. Imagine pairing an A.J. Green with an Andre Johnson? Or a Demaryuis Thomas and a Alshon Jeffrey? That would instantly put your team in the scoring driver's seat and take pressure off finding a third wideout until much later in the draft. This is a group that is growing by the day as far as fantasy football-worthy players but if you fall short addressing this area, you could be in big trouble right away.

1. Calvin Johnson: Simply the best no questions asked. A man among boys when it comes to the wide receiver fraternity, Johnson absolutely is worth of being the number two player off the board behind Peyton Manning, so dominant are his yearly numbers. There is no denying however that Johnson's stats slid more than a little last season as he missed two games with a knee injury and endured a miserable December by quarterback Matthew Stafford. Still an "off year" by Johnson resulted in 84 catches for 1,492 yards and 12 touchdowns which would be a career-year for almost everybody else. Last season's numbers are the worst case scenario, while the best case are the 122-catch/1,964 video game numbers Johnson collected in 2012. No need to overthink anything here as Johnson is as good as it gets.

PROJECTION: 101 catchers 1,726 yards 14 TD

2. A.J. Green: Talk about being consistently excellent, the Cincinnati Bengals' star receiver in 2013 virtually matched his excellent numbers from 2012. Green caught one more pass (98-97) and the same 11 touchdowns last season as he did just a year prior. As a bonus Green threw in a career-high in yardage with 1,426. While a notch below Johnson in overall potency, Green is a monster receiver whose ultra-consistency makes him among the safest of picks in the late round1/early round 2 realm.

PROJECTION: 99 catches 1,398 yards 12 TD

3. Demaryuis Thomas: The Denver Broncos' number 1 receiver certainly did his part in helping Peyton Manning compile his utterly ridiculous passing stats last season. Thomas caught a team-best 92 passes for 1,430 yards and 14 touchdowns as he solidified his place as one of the best number 1 receivers in all of football. With Eric Decker and his high allotment of touchdowns now in New York with the Jets, Thomas could actually increase his already tremendous scoring total by a few more this season to go with the rest of his stellar numbers. A 100-catch season could be in line for Thomas in 2014 so don't hesitate to make him the top pick of your team late in round 1.

PROJECTION: 98 receptions 1,501 yards 15 TD

4. Dez Bryant: Right along the lines of A.J. Green, the Dallas Cowboys' All-Pro wide receiver virtually replicated the breakout stats he accumulated in 2012. All told Bryant has caught 92 and 93 balls to go with 12 and 13 touchdowns in each of the last two seasons respectively, placing himself solidly into the top tier of fantasy football wideouts. A slight separation from Demaryuis Thomas exists due to the volatility and behavioral issues with Bryant but on ability alone they are almost an identical match.

PROJECTION: 92 receptions 1,288 yards 12 TD

5. Antonio Brown: The best recommendation we made in the entire 2013 Fantasy Sports Boss NFL Draft Guide was telling all of you to reach high for Pittsburgh Steelers emerging wide receiver Antonio Brown who was looking at a big time breakout season replacing the departed Mike Wallace. Brown even blew away our lofty expectations as he finished second in the NFL in receptions with 110 to go with 1,499 yards and 8 touchdowns., The Brown-Ben Roethlisberger connection was unstoppable at times despite opposing defenses knowing what was coming. It will be tough for Brown to replicate such awesome production and you never want to pay for a career season but there is no reason he at least can't catch 90 passes for 1,200 yards and around 7 scores. We would take that "diminished" production as an anchor for our wide receivers.

PROJECTION: 102 receptions 1,401 yards 9 TD

6. Brandon Marshall: The incredible breakout of second-year WR Alshon Jeffery was one of the biggest fantasy football storylines of the season in 2013 but it didn't prevent Brandon Marshall from once again putting up top tier numbers himself Truth be told Marshall did lose 18 catches from the year prior (118 to 100) and gave back a decent amount of yardage (1,508 to 1,295) but Jay Cutler's best receiving friend set the bar so high in 2012 that last season's numbers were still terrific no matter how much of an impact Jeffery had on the offense. Josh McCown seemed to favor throwing to Jeffery when Jay Cutler was out and the reverse was true when Cutler was healthy. As long as Cutler can stay on the field, Marshall should once again threaten the 100 catch-mark with close to double-digits in scores.

PROJECTION: 103 receptions 1,311 yards 12 TD

7. Julio Jones: On talent alone the Atlanta Falcons' Julio Jones is as good as any other wide receiver not named Calvin Johnson. However unlike the names listed above, Jones is also the most injury-prone when it comes to the consensus number 1 fantasy football wideouts. A broken foot finished Jones after only 5 games in 2013 which took some of the shine off of his magical 2012 campaign (79 catches/1,198 yards/10 TD's). Don't pay for a full schedule out of Jones as he has had rampant injury problems going back to his days with Alabama but he will come at a discount this season which turn out to be a steal if he can at least log 14 starts.

PROJECTION: 86 receptions 1,172 yards 9 TD

8. Alshon Jeffery: There wasn't a better wide receiver value in all of fantasy football a year ago as the second-year Jeffery exploded with 89 catches for 1,421 yards and 7 touchdowns. Jeffery was on the highlight reels weekly with spectacular catch after spectacular catch and his blend of size and speed is an impossible matchup for opposing defenses to deal with. A good chunk of Jeffery's numbers came when Josh McCown was at quarterback for the Bears and Jay Cutler remains an avowed Brandon Marshall junkie so a slight regression in stats is possible. However there is room for two number 1 fantasy football wide receivers on the same team and the fact Jeffery will come a full round cheaper than Marshall could make him the overall better value.

PROJECTION: 84 receptions 1,284 yards 8 TD

9. Keenan Allen: The rookie third-round pick out of California became an instant star in 2013 as a dearth of receivers on the San Diego Chargers opened the door for Keenan Allen to become the number 1 target of Phillip Rivers. After taking a few weeks to find his footing, Allen performed like a number 1 wideout the rest of the way in catching 71 balls for 1,046 yards and 8 touchdowns. He was particularly tough in the red zone with his good but not great 6-2 size and since the Chargers once again lack top flight weapons, Allen should be busy once again. A borderline WR 1 with some remaining upside.

PROJECTION: 88 receptions 1,102 yards 9 TD

10. Pierre Garcon: Tough to imagine anyone predicting Pierre Garcon would lead the NFL in receptions prior to last season but that is just what the Redskins wideout did in catching 113 balls for 1,346 yards and 5 touchdowns. Having dealt with rampant foot injuries throughout his career, Garcon finally stayed healthy as he turned into the clear favorite target of QB Robert Griffin III. Help is on the way though in the form of DeSean Jackson who came over as a free agent signee and that should take some pressure off of Garcon. Jackson's arrival does figure to take away some of Garcon's numbers in the form of receptions and yardage but the biggest worry we have here is the guy's health which is always a bit dicey. It is tough to imagine the slight Garcon having a second consecutive healthy season given what we have seen in the past and again you never want to pay for a career year. We like Garcon but through all of those receptions last season only five went for scores. In addition Garcon has never caught more than six touchdowns in any given year so there are clear limitations here to be aware of.

PROJECTION: 88 receptions 1,104 yards 5 TD

11. Jordy Nelson: It was a typical year for Green Bay's number 1 receiver in 2013 as Nelson combined a good but not over the top amount of receptions (85) with a very good touchdown total (8). Where Nelson really excels every season is in the yardage department as he has topped 1,250 in two of the last three years and with heavy touchdown target James Jones now in Oakland, an uptick in scores is likely as well in 2014. Flat in his prime years, only injury can stop Nelson from a borderline WR 1 season.

PROJECTION: 91 receptions 1,318 yards 11 TD

12. Victor Cruz: It was a bit of a letdown season for the New York Giants' big play receiver in 2013 as Victor Cruz missed the first two games in his career with injury, failed to reach the 1,000 yard mark since becoming a starter, and seeing his touchdown total drop from 10 to 4. Surely not the WR 1 numbers Cruz' owners were looking for to say the least. The Giants offense was a complete mess last season and under the new leadership of Ben McAdoo, things should click on a higher level in 2014 as Cruz reprises his role as the leading receiver for Eli Manning. As far as Cruz is concerned, he has yet to catch 90 passes in a season but his first two years in the league showed his big-play ability as he grabbed 9 and than 10 scoring throws. Very similar to Jordy Nelson in every way as a low end WR 1.

PROJECTION: 89 receptions 1,221 yards 10 TD

13. Randall Cobb: A fractured tibia in his right leg kept Randall Cobb from having that explosive breakout season that many had anticipated in 2013. The jack-of-all-trades speedster only was able to play in six games where he caught 31 passes for 433 yards. Showing his knack for the big play however, Cobb hauled in 4 touchdowns, a number that is expected to approach double-digits in 2014 health permitting. The Packers have big plans for Cobb this season and he retains massive appeal in all formats since he can also contribute in the running and return game to go with a possible 90 receptions and 1,200 yards. Chalk up the broken tibia to a freak injury and go back to the well aggressively here.

PROJECTION: 88 receptions 1,082 yards 9 TD

14. Wes Welker: Yeah Wes Welker was not in New England anymore. After catching 100 or more passes in five of the last six season, it was a different story in 2013 during Welker's first year with the Denver Broncos as Peyton Manning once again showed his proclivity for spreading the ball around. In addition more concussion problems cost Welker three games which netted him a total of only 73 receptions for 778 yards. The 10 touchdowns Welker scored were terrific but there are some red flags to be concerned about. For one, the next concussion Welker suffers could be his last. Having been diagnosed with two in a four-week span last season, there were some whispers that Welker's family was growing concerned about him playing football going forward. Even moving beyond that risk, Welker no longer figures to be a 100-catch guy as the setup of the Bronco offense is not as reliant on one guy like New England's was. As much as we loved owning Welker in the past, the risk is starting to outweigh the payoff. Pass.

PROJECTION: 91 receptions 1,109 yards 9 TD

15. Vincent Jackson: While there is no denying Vincent Jackson's standing as one of the best big-play receivers in the NFL, his inconsistency from game-to-game is something that can tough to stomach. In any two-week span Jackson is liable to catch 10 balls for 140 yards and two touchdowns and immediately follow that up with a 4-catch outing for 45 yards. Jackson has never caught more than last season's 78 passes in his 10-year career so he has more value in standard leagues than in PPR. However Jackson has caught 24 touchdowns the last three years which again speaks to his big-play ability. Grade Jackson out as a low end WR 1 in standard formats and a 2 in PPR leagues.

PROJECTION: 75 receptions 1,267 yards 9 TD

16. Andre Johnson: Age doesn't seem to be anything but a number to the Houston Texans' Andre Johnson as he comes off a 109-catch season for 1,407 yards and 5 touchdowns. One of the best receivers of his generation and also one of the better PPR fantasy football wideouts in history, Johnson continues to find ways to constantly get open and get his hands on a boatload of passes. A couple of things to be aware of: one is that Johnson will be 33 when the 2014 season begins which is getting up there for a receiver. The second is that Johnson will have the arm-challenged Ryan Fitzpatrick under center which could make it a big challenge in trying to stay above the 100-catch mark. Johnson also have a long history of leg injuries but he has managed to record two straight 16-game campaigns. Finally as great a career as Johnson has had, he has unbelievably never had a double-digit TD season and in the last two years has caught only 2, 4, and 5 scoring passes. With Fitzpatrick now in town, and an increased risk of injury, Johnson should be graded as a WR 2 in all setups.

PROJECTION: 92 receptions 1,238 yards 7 TD

17. Roddy White: Despite going into the 2014 season as a 32-year-old and coming off an injury-ruined campaign the year prior, the Atlanta Falcons still believe longtime star receiver Roddy White has something left to give as they have held extension talks over the winter. Coming off a three-year stretch where he caught 115, 100, and 92 passes as a PPR gem, White plummeted to only 63 receptions in 2013 as he missed 3 games with a hamstring injury and saw Julio Jones replace him as the number 1 receiver in

September. Once White returned to optimal health, he turned back into his old self as he finished in monster fashion. Starting with the team's Dec. 1 game against the Buffalo Bills, White caught 43 balls and two touchdowns in the last five games. White is aging however and so more health woes have to be factored into his draft price. In addition Jones himself is back and healthy for the time being which means he will continue to be Matt Ryan's number 1 big-play wideout. Moving White down to WR 2 status sounds about right.

PROJECTION: 81 receptions 1,182 yards 7 TD

18. T.Y. Hilton: The season-ending torn ACL suffered by veteran Colts wideout Reggie Wayne opened the door for second-year speedster T.Y. Hilton to emerge into a star last season, catching 82 balls for 1,083 yards and 5 touchdowns. Capable of going from 0 to 60 in a nanosecond, Hilton is primed to be one of the next big-play downfield threats and his increasing rapport with Andrew Luck portends to many good times ahead. Upside ceiling play who could cement status as a WR 1 this season.

PROJECTION: 87 receptions 1,126 yards 7 TD

19. Larry Fitzgerald: There is little point in debating the fact that Larry Fitzgerald has slid from his previous perch as one of the best receivers in football. In fact Fitzgerald may no longer be the best wideout on his own team given the emergence of Michael Floyd last season. Be that as it may, the aging (31) but still very effective Fitzgerald grades out as a top WR 2 capable of between 80-90 receptions and around 1,000 yards with double-digits possible in scores. Fitzgerald has failed to reach the 1,000 yard receiving mark in each of the last two seasons though and his last three reception totals have been 80, 71, and 82 which speaks to the fall from his once lofty perch.

PROJECTION: 88 receptions 957 yards 9 TD

20. Julian Edelman: Meet the new Wes Welker. In seamlessly replacing his former teammate in the slot, the similarly skilled Julian Edelman had a monster breakout season with 105 receptions for 1,056 yards and 6 scores. Danny Amendola, Aaron Dobson, and Kenbrell Thompkins are all back and healthy for now but Edelman figures to once again dominate the receptions tally for the Patriots. We want to see Edelman do it again before we anoint him as a WR 1 in PPR formats but he can be graded as a top 2 there, while dropping down to a 3 in standard setups given the light TD total.

PROJECTION: 93 receptions 993 yards 6 TD

21. Michael Crabtree: A torn Achillies tendon suffered at the end of the 2012 season kept Michael Crabtree out of the San Francisco 49ers' offensive plans until the last five games of the regular season when he was eased back into action. Now a full season and a half removed from the surgery, Crabtree should be back to his old self physically and the former 10th overall pick of the 2009 draft should be up for reprising his role as the number 1 wideout for Colin Kaepernick. The 85 catches for 1,105 yards and 9 touchdowns Crabtree caught in 2012 should be what is in play for this season which means he grades out as a WR 2 in all formats.

PROJECTION: 84 receptions 1,089 yards 8 TD

22. Michael Floyd: Floyd is our pick as the best bet to do an Alshon Jeffery 2013 bustout this season after the former Notre Dame standout started to put it all together a year ago. In catching 65 passes for 1,041 yards and 5 touchdowns, Floyd didn't exactly explode but he showed the potential to be a WR 1 as soon as this year. The best part about Floyd only catching those 65 passes in 2013 is that it kept his draft price from getting out of control, thus a big payoff can still be had. We firmly believe Floyd passes Larry Fitzgerald for good as the Arizona Cardinals' number 1 receiver much in the same way Julio Jones did to Roddy White with the Atlanta Falcons. Reach a round early here if you have to do so.

PROJECTION: 81 receptions 1,246 yards 10 TD

23. Marques Colston: There were some very disturbing signs from longtime New Orleans Saints number 1 wide receiver Marques Colston in 2013 as age looks like it is starting to become a part of his statistical equation. Colston lost 8 receptions, 211 yards, and 5 touchdowns from the year before and at 32-years-old, further slippage could be in the offing. There is a decent history of leg injuries for Colston and that risk will only grow as he turns another year older. We have likely reached the point where it is time to jump off this once high-powered scoring train.

PROJECTION: 79 receptions 1,001 yards 7 TD

24. Reggie Wayne: Returning from a torn ACL is a rough injury to come back from for any player but this is especially true for an aging wide receiver as Indianapolis Colts veteran Reggie Wayne is. Having engineered a comeback season for the ages in 2012 when he caught 106 passes for 1,355 yards, Wayne will be faced with a ton of questions heading into training camp about whether he has lost a step or two and can be somewhat the player he once was. With T.Y. Hilton having ascended to near-WR 1 status, there is not as much pressure on Wayne to be the go-to-guy anymore but in fantasy football terms this could be a dicey proposition. Wayne was habitually one of the hardest-working and fit athletes in the game before the injury and no doubt he will put himself in the best physical shape he can for his return. However we smell a decline coming and it may not be pretty. Like with other aging receivers, you have to know when to ignore the name and accept what the current situation tells you.

PROJECTION: 71 receptions 802 yards 4 TD

25. Cordarelle Patterson: We would be feeling so much more excitement for the Minnesota Vikings' Cordarelle Patterson if not for the fact his team has some of the biggest quarterback question marks in the entire NFL. Whether it is rookie Teddy Bridgewater or in the incompetent Matt Cassel taking snaps from under center, the incredibly gifted Patterson will have a tough time realizing his vast potential this season. It came in only flashes but Patterson showed as a rookie in 2013 that he is capable of scoring from anywhere on the field when he gets the football in his hands. Unfortunately Patterson can't throw the ball to himself which speaks to the limits on his upside. The numbers will no doubt trend upwards though so don't let Patterson idly slip by in the draft. Just don't overpay for him either thinking a massive breakout is on the way.

PROJECTION: 70 receptions 888 yards 7 TD

26. Percy Harvin: One measly game and one measly catch was all that both the Seattle Seahawks and Percy Harvin's fantasy football owners got out of the multi-dimensional wideout in 2013. Living up fully to his injury prone label, Harvin dealt with a serious hip issue which was followed by a concussion that pretty much wiped out his entire year. When on the field few are as exciting and productive as Harvin. However few are also more injury-prone which is why we always strongly advise against drafting players like this who can't stay on the field. Harvin is a perpetual tease who is not worth the trouble.

PROJECTION: 65 receptions 798 yards 6 TD

27. DeSean Jackson: Whether or not the Philadelphia Eagles used it as an excuse to appease the public, the team didn't bat an eye in cutting the mouthy but big-play DeSean Jackson in the offseason due to his possible association with gangs. Not to choosing to believe the rumor, the Washington Redskins quickly swooped in and grabbed Jackson to team up with Pierre Garcon to give the team a very potent pair of receivers. We continue to believe that Jackson is one of the more overrated players in all of fantasy football as it took the arrival of Chip Kelly's crazy passing offense for him to finally reach the 80-catch mark. Jackson's strength lies in picking up yardage with deep routes and scoring a solid amount of touchdowns. He figures to take a step back from the career year he had in 2013 as Jackson goes to a Washington offense that is not even in the same room as the Eagles' unit. Once again Jackson's name outpaces his actual production and he squarely falls into the wide receiver 3 region as a result.

PROJECTION: 72 receptions 1,206 yards 6 TD

28. Kendall Wright: Few probably realize just how good second-year Tennessee Titans wideout Kendall Wright was in 2013 as he caught 94 passes for 1,079 yards with mediocre passers in Jake Locker and Ryan Fitzpatrick throwing him the football. Wright only has to add to his woefully low 2 touchdown total to reach his optimum efficiency and if he can get that number to at least the 5 mark, you are looking at a top end WR 2. It would be tough to think he could replicate those 94 catches with Locker back under center however so keep expectations somewhat in check.

PROJECTION: 88 receptions 1,037 yards 5 TD

29. Golden Tate: Golden Tate's four season tenure with the Seattle Seahawks, who drafted him in the second round back in 2010 out of Notre Dame, could be categorized in the solid but unspectacular realm. Oftentimes Tate would have a monster game once a month and than go back into hiding the other three weeks. His high in receptions was last season's 64 and Tate will play the clear second fiddle to Calvin Johnson in Detroit. A WR 3 at best and that only goes for standard formats.

PROJECTION: 68 receptions 905 yards 5 TD

30. Mike Wallace: While Wallace did catch a career-high 73 balls in his first season with the Miami Dolphins, he caught only 5 touchdowns and was completely invisible at times after inking that mammoth free-agent contract. A big finish helped Wallace net 930 receiving yards which is not a number to scoff at but the overall package was disappointing, especially when you consider how much Miami was paying him to put up WR 1 numbers. Ryan Tannehill is on a solid upward plane in his development however and the two seemed much more in sync as the season went on. If the Miami offensive line can buy Tannehill more time, Wallace will benefit from some more big plays down the field and thus a push past the 1,000 yard receiving mark is likely. There is some bounce back appeal here at a much cheaper draft price so we are inclined to revisit Wallace as a WR 3 with upside again.

PROJECTION: 75 receptions 1,032 yards 8 TD

31. Torrey Smith: It was another solid step forward in production for Baltimore Ravens number 1 receiver Torrey Smith in 2013 as he firmly became the team's top target in the passing game with Anquan Boldin having left town prior to the season. Still Smith didn't exactly jump off the map with his production as some expected, catching only 65 passes and 4 touchdowns. The 1,128 yards was a big number and if Smith can start pairing his excellence there with some more receptions, the results could be knocking on WR 1 territory in standard formats. Right now Smith checks in as a WR 2 in standard league and a WR 3 in PPR with remaining upside.

PROJECTION: 73 receptions 1,177 yards 8 TD

32. Eric Decker: Participating in an offense that will go down in NFL history as the most potent single-season unit ever certainly was a nice way for wide receiver Eric Decker to head into free agency. Decker parlayed an 87 catch/1,288 yard/11 TD campaign into a massive free agent haul from the New York Jets where he will be the team's number 1 wideout for second-year QB Geno Smith. The dropoff from Peyton Manning to Smith at quarterback is the size of the Grand Canyon and so expecting Decker to come close to his numbers the last two seasons would be foolish. Start by cutting the touchdown total in half, while also chopping about 200 yards in receiving as well. It will be interesting to see how Decker performs not having Demaryuis Thomas and Wes Welker drawing defenders away from his side of the field. We like Decker but not as anything more than a WR 3 in all formats given the massive drop in the offensive potency of his QB.

PROJECTION: 79 receptions 1,082 yards 7 TD

33. Jeremy Maclin: The Eagles brought back the free agent Maclin on a one-year deal despite their former first round pick failing to make it out of training camp due to a torn ACL last season. While Maclin has yet to live up to his lofty draft status, he has also not gotten a chance to see how his skills translate to Chip Kelly's incredible offense. With DeSean Jackson out of the picture, there are plenty of balls left over to be caught. Maclin has the chance to be a monster late round pick since he will enter camp 100 percent healthy and ready to put his stamp on the Kelly passing attack. Don't forget about him.

PROJECTION: 77 receptions 915 yards 7 TD

34. Terrance Williams: The Cowboys seemed to hit on the third-round pick they invested on Baylor wideout Terrance Williams in the 2013 NFL Draft as the rookie showed some very intriguing big-play ability to the tune of 44 catches for 736 yards and 5 scores. Consistency was not part of the equation though as Williams went the Golden Tate route of having as monster game one week and than completely vanishing the next. A full offseason of workouts and complete training camp should help smooth out the rough edges however. Williams can be a cheap WR 3 investment that could pay off nicely given what we have already seen and the potential that remains.

PROJECTION: 65 receptions 882 yards 6 TD

35. Cecil Shorts: In the wasteland for offensive talent that is Jacksonville, wide receiver Cecil Shorts has been the one guy who performed like a solid fantasy football weapon since becoming a starter in 2012. It was during that season when Shorts announced his arrival with a 7-TD campaign to go with 55 receptions for 979 yards despite having to deal with quite possibly the worst quarterback play in the league. Things didn't get much better on the passing front last season either as both Chad Henne and Blaine Gabbert fell on their faces despite Shorts upping his receptions total to 66. With another rookie QB arriving in Blake Bortles, more struggles in the passing game are expected for the Jaguars which will negatively impact Shorts' value. This is a WR 3 all the way but ideally you would like to draft Shorts as your top backup if possible.

PROJECTION: 67 receptions 825 yards 6 TD

36. Dwayne Bowe: It was another mediocre season for longtime Kansas City Chiefs wide receiver Dwayne Bowe in 2013 as the arrival of veteran Alex Smith failed to elevate his numbers. Altogether Bowe caught 57 balls for 673 yards and 5 touchdowns which are borderline WR 3 numbers in fantasy football terms. In addition Bowe got busted for marijuana possession in the offseason which means he is dangerously close to being suspended by the league. No thank you. His best days are now clearly in the rearview mirror.

PROJECTION: 61 receptions 798 yards 6 TD

37. Riley Cooper: Off-the-field controversies aside, there was no denying the chemistry that quarterback Nick Foles and WR Riley Cooper had once the former became the Philadelphia Eagles' starter in place of the injured Michael Vick. Showing a knack for making big plays deep, Cooper racked up 8 receiving touchdowns and 835 yards on only 47 receptions. The low receptions total will surely go up; possibly by more than a little as DeSean Jackson is now a Washington Redskin and Jeremy Maclin is making his way back from injury. Cooper is still best served as a standard league receiver due to the lack of top end receptions which leaves him coming up a bit short in PPR formats. There does appear to be more to see here however.

PROJECTION: 65 receptions 921 yards 9 TD

38. Anquan Boldin: Despite entering into the 2014 season at the advanced age of 34, San Francisco 49ers wide receiver Anquan Boldin shows little signs of slippage. Getting out of Baltimore and their run-heavy offense was a godsend for Boldin as he shot back up over the 80-catch mark (85) in his first season with the 49ers, while also exploding for 1,179 yards and 7 touchdowns. In short Boldin turned out to be one of the better value plays last season as he and Colin Kaepernick got on the same page right off the bat. The return of Michael Crabtree complicates things just a bit entering 2014 however and the 49ers also rely heavily on the run so there may not be enough footballs to go around for Boldin to stay above the 80-catch mark. Still this is a guy in tip top shape with solid durability to his name which makes an investment here not very risky considering the age. We bet there is one more decent season left in the tank at WR 3 prices.

PROJECTION: 77 receptions 1,093 yards 7 TD

39. Hakeem Nicks: Boy has this guy's career taken a nosedive straight into the toilet the last two seasons. Spanning 2010 and 2011, Hakeem Nicks was showing himself to be one of the best receivers in football. Nicks would go over 1,000 yards receiving in each of those two seasons while also grabbing 11 and 7 touchdowns respectively. Unfortunately Nicks' pronounced knack for getting injured got in the way of his rise to stardom as rampant ankle/leg/toe injuries cost the Giants' wideout three games in 2012 and another one in 2013. Even when Nicks was on the field the last two seasons, his numbers plummeted as he looked a step slow and showcased terrible body language amid reports there was a rift between him and the coaching staff. The bottom fell out last season when Nicks caught only 56 passes and failed to get into the end zone even once. The Giants showed no interest in bringing him back and instead Nicks was forced to settle for a one-year deal in a crowded Indianapolis Colts receiving corps with T.Y. Hilton and Reggie Wayne both ahead of him on the depth chart. There is little to like about Nicks at this point other than his QB. The injuries, sliding performance, and crowed receiver ranks make him nothing more than a bench guy at best.

PROJECTION: 55 receptions 782 yards 4 TD

40. Danny Amendola: What a shocker. Danny Amendola got hurt again in 2013. There may not be a more injury-prone player in all of football than the New England Patriots wideout who missed four games last season, upping his career total to an incredible 26 in only five years in the league. Amendola was signed to his massive contract to do what Julian Edelman did last season in catching over 100 passes but that will never happen due to the fragile nature of his body. Edelman earned the trust of Tom Brady as the go-to-receiver in the offense and Amendola could only be graded as a WR 3 anyways due to his extreme injury risk.

PROJECTION: 73 receptions 735 yards 4 TD

41. Emmanuel Sanders: Sleeper alert! Any wide receiver who ends up in the Denver Broncos offense with Peyton Manning at quarterback is always a prime person of interest and that clearly is the case with Emmanuel Sanders who signed on as a free agent from Pittsburgh. Coming off his best season in 2013 as a starter opposite Antonio Brown, Sanders caught 67 passes for 740 yards and 6 touchdowns. With Eric Decker leaving town for the New York Jets also as a free agent, Sanders figures to slide right in opposite Demaryuis Thomas on the opposite side of the field which means potentially plentiful touchdowns and another career-high in receptions. The best is yet to come with Sanders and he could turn out to be the cheapest double-digit receiver in fantasy football this season.

PROJECTION: 79 receptions 994 yards 9 TD

42. James Jones: One of the more underrated receivers in football the last two seasons, James Jones no doubt used his prime position in the explosive Green Bay Packers passing attack to cash in as a free agent with the Oakland Raiders. Unfortunately for Jones, Rodgers won't be going along for the ride and instead he will be catching passes from the suddenly shaky Matt Schaub. Having caught 17 touchdowns the last two seasons, Jones knows how to get into the end zone which makes him a solid WR 3 in standard formats. His career-high in receptions is only 64 though so his upside is very limited in PPR leagues. A guy who won't command a heavy price in the draft, Jones is a nice bench guy who could help during bye weeks.

PROJECTION: 67 receptions 835 yards 7 TD

43. Marvin Jones: The propensity for opposing defenses to shift double-coverage to the side of the field where All-Pro WR A.J. Green roamed allowed Marvin Jones to announce his arrival to the NFL with a 10-TD season in 2013 on the opposite side of the field. Jones quickly became a favorite red zone target of QB Andy Dalton, especially during the second half of the year. Now entering his third season in the league, Jones has a bit more room to improve which makes him a somewhat attractive investment. However Green will continue to dominate the receptions haul, pushing Jones to standard league usage only.

PROJECTION: 61 receptions 809 yards 9 TD

44. DeAndre Hopkins: Before there was Sammy Watkins, Clemson's wideouts were led by big-play speedster DeAndre Hopkins. Unfortunately for Hopkins, the incessant QB struggles that the Houston Texans dealt with last season between Matt Schaub and rookie Case Keenum, didn't allow for the kind of rookie breakout some expected. Altogether Hopkins caught 52 balls for an impressive 802 yards, he scored only twice. With veteran Ryan

Fitzpatrick and his lack of deep ball arm strength coming to town, Hopkins' best trait as a downfield threat is a bit neutered. In addition Andre Johnson remains the clear number 1 receiver in the Texans offense so Hopkins' immediate future is not looking so promising.

PROJECTION: 62 receptions 955 yards 5 TD

45. Aaron Dobson: The rookie second-round pick out of Marshall looks like a very nice addition to the New England receiving unit. Despite fellow rookie Kenbrell Thompkins getting all the early pub, it was Dobson who eventually overtook his teammate as a starting wideout. Things didn't go completely according to plan for Dobson however as he missed four games with injuries and grabbed only 37 passes for 519 yards and 4 scores. There is a crying need for a deep playmaker on the New England offense and Dobson is the most-equipped to fill that role right from the start. While we are not saying Dobson will go all Randy Moss on opposing defenses, he does stand a solid chance of putting up fantasy football-friendly stats at a very affordable draft price.

PROJECTION: 65 receptions 798 yards 6 TD

46. Tavon Austin: All of those footballs that Tavon Austin caught in college with West Virginia failed to come over for the trip to the NFL in 2013. The rookie only showed his dynamic ability every so often and the cumulative totals of 40 receptions for 418 yards and 4 scores came up quite a bit short of expectations. Austin has dynamic ability though and the Rams no doubt will make sure he gets the ball much more often this season. The sleeper hype has died down so Austin's draft price will come very cheap. A potentially large payoff awaits.

PROJECTION: 68 receptions 837 yards 6 TD

47. Steve Smith: After 11 seasons with the Carolina Panthers where he set all sorts of receiving records, Steve Smith was let go by the only organization he has ever played for since the team drafted him in the third round of the 2001 NFL Draft. At 35-years-old, Smith has lost more than a step but he should be able to carve out one more WR 3 season in standard formats for the Baltimore Ravens. One of the most intense players in all of football, Smith will do whatever he has to do to succeed but investing in receivers over the age of 33 is always a bad idea.

PROJECTION: 61 receptions 756 yards 5 TD

48. Reuben Randle: It will be interesting to see which LSU receiver grabs hold of the number 2 spot for the New York Giants this season. Second-year man Reuben Randle figures to have the upper hand on rookie Odell Beckham Jr. but this is one competition worth watching. With Hakeem Nicks hobbling and playing at half speed for most of the 2013 season, Randle played extensively as a rookie where he showed some big-play ability in catching 41 passes for 611 yards and 6 touchdowns. Victor Cruz will lead the Giants in receiving in 2014 but at 6-2 and 208 pounds, Randle has a chance to be a very good red zone weapon which will boost him in standard formats. Right now Randle is just a bench guy with upside.

PROJECTION: 59 receptions 733 yards 6 TD

49. Kenny Stills: The rookie fifth round pick out of Oklahoma made the most out of his 32 receptions in 2013, as five of them went for scores. Stills is just the latest New Orleans Saints receiver to make his presence felt in their annually explosive offense. As always however, Drew Brees spreads the football around which makes each receiver tough to depend on from week-to-week given the volatility of their production. Stills is interesting as a late-round play but don't go overboard.

PROJECTION: 44 receptions 678 yards 6 TD

50. Greg Jennings: Life without Aaron Rodgers as your quarterback was much tougher for former Pro Bowl wideout Greg Jennings during his first season with the Minnesota Vikings in 2013. With the woeful Christian Ponder and the average Matt Cassel under center, Jennings caught only 4 touchdown passes among his 68 receptions and he also failed to reach the 1,000-yard receiving mark which he did three times with the Green Bay Packers. Jennings is not likely going to see much improvement if any this season what with either Cassel or rookie Teddy Bridgewater calling the signals at QB.

PROJECTION: 70 receptions 915 yards 5 TD

51. Stevie Johnson: The former 7th round pick made good by the Buffalo Bills found himself in a new locale this offseason after being dealt during the NFL Draft to the San Francisco 49ers. It was an odd move for the 49ers since they already had Michael Crabtree and Anquan Boldin. Despite having to deal with some of the worst quarterbacking in the NFL over the last five years, Johnson managed to make himself into a very solid receiver, with three 1,000 yard campaigns in a row until injuries forced him to miss four games last season. Despite the knack for the big play, Johnson has only crossed the 80-catch mark once in his six-year career and he could actually be the third wideout behind Boldin and Crabtree in a run-oriented offense. While Johnson in the past was a top end WR 3, this season he is on the border of that level given his new surroundings.

PROJECTION: 63 receptions 826 yards 6 TD

52. Brian Hartline: The Miami Dolphins' Brian Hartline might have caught the quietest 74 and 76 passes the last two seasons. A very dependable and smart slot receiver, Hartline served as the security blanket during that time for green QB Ryan Tannehill. Despite going past the 1,000 yard mark in each of the last two seasons, to go along with the 70-plus receptions, Harline showed his limitations by catching only five total touchdowns during that span. Mike Wallace will be the main target in the red zone so Hartline is limited in the value he brings to standard formats. He makes the grade as a low end WR 3 in PPR formats however.

PROJECTION: 78 receptions 1,026 yards 4 TD

53. Jarrett Boykin: With James Jones having missed time last season with injury, the door swung wide open for second-year undrafted wideout Jarrett Boykin to show he could be a viable weapon in the passing offense. Boykin was an instant hit, catching 49 passes for 681 yards and 3 touchdowns in part-time duty. With Jones now an Oakland Raider, Boykin will be the every week third receiver for the Packers. Duplicating the numbers Jones had the last couple of seasons sounds about right.

PROJECTION: 61 receptions 837 yards 5 TD

54. Mike Williams: Williams has as new home in Buffalo with the Bills but his role as a number 2 receiver doesn't change as he will clearly defer to rookie Sammy Watkins. An offseason incident for trespassing was a bit of a red flag and Williams is also coming off an injury-wracked 2013 campaign. This is a bench option at best but considering the awful Bills passing offense and his role as the number 2, there is little to recommend.

PROJECTION: 45 receptions 698 yards 4 TD

56. Rod Streater: It is tough being an Oakland Raiders receiver but Rod Streater made the best of it in 2013 as he caught 60 passes for 888 yards and 4 touchdowns despite some of the worst QB play in the league. Streater is the classic big play guy who can help some as a WR 3 in standard formats only. Some more improvement is expected, especially with Matt Schaub under center however.

PROJECTION: 68 receptions 897 yards 5 TD

57. Harry Douglas: The best third receiver in football, Harry Douglas became an overnight smash hit replacing the injured Julio Jones last season for the explosive Atlanta Falcons passing attack. Douglas would catch 85 passes for 1,067 yards but only two touchdowns. With Jones back healthy for 2014, Douglas slides back to his third wideout spot which didn't lend itself to fantasy football-useful numbers prior. However with Tony Gonzalez now in retirement, there are some more passes to go around so Douglas could be a similar case to Jarrett Boykin in Green Bay. Jones of course is never healthy for long so Douglas could turn out to be a monster receiver again all for the cost of a late round pick.

PROJECTION: 48 receptions 678 yards 4 TD

THE REST

58. Doug Baldwin: Could get a longer look with Golden Tate out of town and Sidney Rice always hurt.

59. Andrew Hawkins: Gets a fresh start in WR-needy Cleveland after toiling for three years in Cincinnati. QB issues limit any type of upside.

60. Marlon Brown: Brown really acquitted himself well as a rookie in 2013 with 7 touchdown grabs and 49 catches overall. Could be a decent enough bench option in standard formats.

61. Nate Washington: Underrated receiver has caught as many as 74 balls in a season. The TD option over Kendall Wright in a shaky Tennessee passing offense.

62. Andre Roberts: The Washington Redskins opened the checkbook for the just all right Roberts who caught as many as 64 balls back in 2012 for the Cardinals. Upside worth looking into late.

63. Brandon LaFell: Anyone who signs on with New England and QB Tom Brady has our attention. Caught 49 balls and 5 touchdowns last season with Carolina in a run-heavy offense. Another late round pick who could really surprise due to his new locale.

64. Jerricho Cotchery: Cotchery is being counted on to replace the receptions lost with the free agent defections of both Steve Smith and Brandon LaFell. Scored a career-high 10 touchdowns last season but it has been five years since Cotchery caught more than 57 passes.

65. Jeremy Kerley: The only bright spot on the New York Jets offense last season as the team had quite possibly the worst collection of receivers in the league. Backup option in PPR leagues as the Jets like to use him out of the slot area as a safety valve for Geno Smith.

66. Chris Givens: Entering his third season in the league, Chris Givens has shown nothing but flashes of ability in a shaky Rams passing offense. Leave on the wire.

67. Jerrel Jernigan: The former third round pick did next to nothing his first three years in the league until given a late starting role in place of an injured Victor Cruz in December. Jernigan caught 19 passes and 2 touchdowns the last three games of the season which opened eyes. The Giants drafted Odell Beckham in the first round of the draft however which calls into questions Jernigan's spot in the offense with Cruz and also Reuben Randle both ahead of him on the depth chart.

68. Nate Burleson: Burleson suffered one of the more odd injuries of the 2013 season when he broke his arm in a car accident caused by him trying to stop pizzas from falling off his seat. Burleson has a nice opportunity as a prime receiver alongside Jerricho Cotchery in Cleveland but more offseason injuries cloud his future.

69. Kenny Britt: The Tennessee Titans finally tired of all of Kenny Britt's off-the-field negatives and penchant for injuries. No one doubts Britt's nose for the end zone but until he stays on the field and acts like an adult, he is nothing but wire fodder.

70. Kenbrell Thompkins: The undrafted rookie looked like a monster find for the New England Patriots last season in September after Danny Amendola got injured yet again. Thompkins caught some early touchdowns from Tom Brady but eventually he was passed by fellow rookie Aaron Dobson on the depth chart, not to mention Amendola and Julian Edelman. Worth another look due to the location but this is not nearly as exciting a story as it was early last season.

71. Lance Moore: Moore has always been a nice player to own in fantasy football due to his presence on one of the more explosive passing offenses in football with the New Orleans Saints but his numbers tended to fluctuate wildly from game to game. Moore has a new home in Pittsburgh with a Steelers team that is throwing the football more than ever so he retains decent value. A borderline WR 3.

72. Denarius Moore: Moore has caught at least 45 balls and 5 touchdowns in each of the last two seasons for the Oakland Raiders which is nothing to sneeze at. However with James Jones joining Rod Streater, Moore is now the third receiver on the team which is not a good thing on the awful Raiders.

73. Mohamed Sanu: Sanu became a name of notice last season by catching 47 passes for 455 yards and 2 touchdowns. The Bengals have fallen in love throwing the football so Sanu could sneak in as a bench wideout option due to being behind A.J. Green and Marvin Jones.

74. Sidney Rice: Enough chasing that one big season Rice had with Brett Favre while with the Minnesota Vikings because it is never coming back. Rice is one of the biggest injury-risk players in the game so no need to try this again.

75. Stephen Hill: Could catch the odd touchdown but Eric Decker's arrival pushed Hill down to wire status. On a Jets team that can't throw the football well, that is a non-starter in fantasy football terms.

76. Robert Woods: Woods drew attention to his 40 catches last season as a rookie for the Buffalo Bills but the arrival of Sammy Watkins means he is just a bench guy at best.

77. Da'Rick Rogers: Rogers was a talent that fell out of the 2013 draft due to off-the-field issues. Very small sample size but in five games Rogers caught 14 balls for 192 yards and two scores. The Colts are well-stocked with receivers though so Rodgers is just a waiver guy.

78. Marquess Wilson: Wilson is expected to be the third receiver in the all of a sudden potent Chicago Bears passing attack this season. Really just someone to monitor in order to see if Wilson does enough to warrant a tryout.

TIGHT ENDS

Draft Strategy: The proliferation of the pass-catching tight end the last few seasons in fantasy football has gone hand-in-hand with the explosion of the passing offense. The depth here is greater than ever before but there are also some problems right at the top after Jimmy Graham goes off the board. Rob Gronkowski once again figures to miss a portion of the season after tearing his ACL in 2013, this after returning from back surgery. In addition Julius Thomas is a perennial injury-risk, while Jason Witten saw his raw numbers drop for the first time last season. Graham absolutely deserves a late first round grade due to his WR-like numbers. After that it is best to wait until the fourth round or later as there are some prime sleeper values to be had such Jordan Reed, Charles Clay, Tyler Eifert, rookie Eric Ebron, and Levine Toilolo.

1. Jimmy Graham: There is Jimmy Graham and than there is everybody else when it comes to 2014 fantasy football tight ends. This is a guy who puts up WR 1 numbers such as the 16 touchdown grabs on 86 receptions for 1,215 yards last season. There is no one Drew Brees looks to more in the high-powered Saints offense and with Graham still flat in his prime, is set to replicate his 2013 numbers with little effort.

PROJECTION: 88 receptions 1,252 yards 14 TD

2. Julius Thomas: Prior to last season's start, we told you all on the website to take a flier on second-year Denver Broncos tight end Julius Thomas after he put up a string of big performances in the exhibition season and also due to the fact his quarterback was some guy named Peyton Manning. The extremely athletic Thomas made good on his sleeper status and than some in 2013 as he caught 65 balls for 788 yards and 12 touchdowns. Thomas was a monster near the red zone and further improvement is very likely as he is just scratching the surface of his ability. The only issue is Thomas' history of leg and ankle injuries which cost him two games a year ago. Thomas has some risk due to his rocky health but otherwise is should be the second tight end off the board.

PROJECTION: 75 receptions 921 yards 12 TD

3. Jordan Cameron: Along the same lines as Julius Thomas last season, third-year Cleveland Browns tight end Jordan Cameron posted a significant breakout by catching 80 passes for 917 yards and 7 scores. Outside of Jimmy Graham, there wasn't a more productive tight end the first month of the season but the numbers leveled off slightly once Josh Gordon returned. However with Gordon now facing a season-long suspension, Cameron should once again be the number 1 target meaning he could actually improve on his numbers across the board. While not the touchdown weapon Thomas is, Cameron is in line to post a Jason Witten-type season where 90 receptions is a possibility.

PROJECTION: 82 receptions 956 yards 8 TD

4. Jason Witten: There are few players we haven't praised more over the years than longtime PPR monster Jason Witten. With 879 career receptions, no one has been more productive outside of the just retired Tony Gonzalez when it comes to raw catches over the last ten years. Witten is aging a bit though as he turns 32 but he remains as good as there is in the NFL at getting open and racking up the catches. Witten did slip to 73 receptions last season which was his lowest total since 2006 but he countered that by catching 8 touchdowns which was his most since 2010. Despite Witten never being a big TD guy, last season notwithstanding, this is a tried-and-true weapon who still has another few big years left in the tank.

PROJECTION: 86 receptions 928 yards 6 TD

5. Vernon Davis: It was the same old solid story for Vernon Davis in 2013. Caught a bunch of touchdowns with 13. Failed to catch a big time total of footballs with only 52. Went over 800 yards receiving with 850. At 30-years-old Davis is right in his prime years which means he should be in the neighborhood of all of those numbers again in 2014. The earlier injury issues Davis had in his career have also become a non-story as he logged five straight years of 16 games before sitting out once last season. Dependable.

PROJECTION: 57 receptions 829 yards 11 TD

6. Rob Gronkowski: For the second season in a row, prospective owners of New England Patriots tight end Rob Gronkowski will have to deal with the All Pro missing games right from the start as he makes his way back from 2013's gruesome torn ACL and MCL. Just a year earlier it was

Gronkowski's recovery from offseason back surgery that had him out until midseason. In the seven games Gronkowski did play in last year, he was his usual excellent self with 4 touchdowns among his 39 receptions. However we are well past the point of Gronkowski being injury-prone and investing here is about as risky as it gets. The potential numbers are no doubt alluring but tight end is filled with upstart options and good depth so your best bet is to avoid Gronkowski and the uncertainty he brings.

PROJECTION: 51 receptions 737 yards 6 TD

7. Dennis Pitta: One of our favorite sleepers prior to 2013 drafts was Baltimore Ravens upstart tight end Dennis Pitta. Reminding us of a young Jason Witten, Pitta unfortunately didn't even make it through the first week of training camp before suffering a serious hip injury. Pitta fought back to return to the field for the last six games of the season where he showed why he was so likable in the first place as he caught 20 balls for 169 yards and a score. Pitta has tremendous hands and can be a terrific red zone target so all the tools are there for a breakout a year later. The best part is that Pitta's draft price will be so much more cheaper this season which means more potential value.

PROJECTION: 75 receptions 810 yards 6 TD

8. Greg Olsen: Few players were as consistent from 2012 through 2013 than Carolina's Greg Olsen. During that span Olsen caught 69 and 73 passes, gathered 843 and 816 yards, and hauled in 5 and 6 touchdowns. With the Panthers saying goodbye to Steve Smith and Brandon LaFell, there is a crying need for prime pass catchers in the Panthers offense which Olsen is very capable of filling. While Olsen is the definition of a solid and steady player, he could inch up the overall numbers again this season due to Cam Newton having to look his way a bit more.

PROJECTION: 77 receptions 836 yards 6 TD

9. Jordan Reed: The rookie third round pick out of Florida was really making a name for himself in 2013 as he showed advanced receiving skills to the tune of 45 catches in only 9 games for 499 yards and 3 scores. Unfortunately a bad concussion prevented Reed from playing the last month of the season. Reed was said to be symptom-free during the winter which means he will be given the chance to hit the ground running as a major part of the Washington Redskins passing game. With Robert Griffin III on the lookout for a safety valve, Reed could be a terrific sleeper candidate.

PROJECTION: 67 receptions 831 yards 5 TD

10. Charles Clay: Yet another 2014 tight end sleeper who could pay off handsomely this season for those who make an investment. With Ryan Tannehill needing a security outlet receiver given how poor his offensive line was, Clay became an integral part of the passing attack as he caught 69 passes for 759 yards and 6 touchdowns. Those numbers alone are tight end 1 worthy and Clay hints he has more to give this season as well. Clay has the perfect setup right now to threaten the 80 reception mark and that would place him squarely among the better tight ends in the game.

PROJECTION: 74 receptions 819 yards 6 TD

11. Antonio Gates: It was a terrific comeback season for San Diego Chargers tight end Antonio Gates in 2013 as he did his part in helping to revive the previously struggling offense by catching 77 balls for 872 yards and 4 touchdowns. The 77 catches were the most Gates has had since 2009 and a lot of that had to do with health as the longtime Pro Bowler played in all 16 games after missing 10 the previous three years. At 34-years-old Gates has lost a step or two which means he no longer is a big downfield target, a responsibility he will cede to Ladarius Green. Also it is foolhardy to expect Gates to stay healthy for 16 games again two seasons in a row so he remains a big risk. At this point Gates' draft price has dropped to the point where it wouldn't be a horrible idea to attempt to get one more season of numbers out of him but we get the sneaking feeling that now is the time to cash in your chips.

PROJECTION: 65 receptions 752 yards 5 TD

12. Zach Ertz: Despite longtime Eagles tight end Brent Celek remaining on the roster, Zach Ertz is clearly both the future and the present for Philadelphia. A former 2013 third round pick out of Stanford, Ertz possesses quite a bit of untapped potential after being underutilized last season as a rookie. Showing a knack for the end zone that went back to his college days, Ertz caught 4 touchdowns on his 36 catches. We all know how much the Eagles love to throw the football under Chip Kelly and Ertz figures to contribute his fair share in 2014 by adding numbers across the board. Another upside play along the lines of Dwight Reed.

PROJECTION: 52 receptions 673 yards 6 TD

13. Kyle Rudolph: It was a rough season in 2013 for Kyle Rudolph who played in only 8 games as he landed on IR with a foot injury. Still in looking for a bright side, Rudolph caught 30 passes for 313 yards and 3 touchdowns in those eight games and if you double those numbers, you have very nice production across the board. Rudolph is one of the best red zone weapons among all tight ends so 7-10 touchdowns is very likely if he can stay in one piece. This is not the place to look for a 70-catch season however so downgrade some in PPR.

PROJECTION: 65 receptions 678 yards 7 TD

14. Martellus Bennett: After inking a sizable free agent deal to leave the New York Giants for the Chicago Bears, Martellus Bennett had his second consecutive career season with 64 catches for 759 yards and 5 scores. With Brandon Marshall and Alshon Jeffery dominating in the passing game, that stat haul is pretty much all we can expect out of Bennett going forward in the Chicago offense however. Still this is a very safe play who won't hurt you but at the same time Bennett doesn't have the upside or ceiling of some of the other guys listed above.

PROJECTION: 62 receptions 810 yards 5 TD

15. Ladarius Green: If only Antonio Gates would just retire already. With all due respect to the longtime San Diego Chargers All Pro tight end, the time is now for third-year upstart Ladarius Green who has the same type of background as a basketball player and possesses tremendous size and speed like his aging teammate. In part-time duty last season, Green showed big play ability with 376 yards on only 17 receptions and 3 scores. With Gates constantly hobbled by injuries, which is an issue that will only grow more stark as he turns another year older, Green could easily pass him in numbers this season. The volatility of playing time and Gates' giant presence leave Green more in the realm of a backup with upside instead of as a starting option.

PROJECTION: 41 receptions 582 yards 5 TD

16. Heath Miller: Miller enters into his 10th season with the Pittsburgh Steelers in 2014 and during that time he has served as the primary safety outlet for QB Ben Roethlisberger, especially near the red zone. Injuries are becoming a part of the picture though as Miller has missed three games over the last two seasons and he has a history of concussions to be concerned with. However when on the field Miller still has it as he comes off a 2013 season where he was on pace to catch the second-most passes of his career. The single receiving touchdown was a bummer no doubt but just a year earlier Miller gathered in eight scores so the first number is an outlier that won't be repeated given the attention he gets from Roethlisberger near the end zone. Miller's draft price is extremely affordable and the very solid numbers he provides make him one of the better buys overall at the position as the fantasy football community looks to the more exciting upstarts. However if you choose to wait on drafting this spot until very late, Miller is the guy to get.

PROJECTION: 61 receptions 658 yards 5 TD

17. Garrett Graham: The Houston Texans had no issue letting longtime tight end Owen Daniels leave via free agency after seeing how well backup Garrett Graham played in his place. Showing terrific hands and solid route running ability, Graham caught 49 balls for 545 yards and 5 touchdowns in only 13 games. Ryan Fitzpatrick is a quarterback who always has liked to throw to the tight end so Graham carries some very good sleeper potential this season. Another guy who you can wait on drafting but who in the end could put up top ten numbers among this group.

PROJECTION: 62 receptions 698 yards 5 TD

18. Delanie Walker: After seven years toiling as a backup tight end for the San Francisco 49ers, Delanie Walker finally got his chance to show what he could do with starter snaps in 2013 after signing as a free agent with the Tennessee Titans. Walker did a more than nice job in catching 60 passes for 571 yards and 6 touchdowns, while serving as a trusted outlet for Jake Locker and Ryan Fitzpatrick. What we saw out of Walker last season is probably the best he has so don't count on anymore elevation in the numbers, especially with either Locker or rookie Tom Savage under center. Walker has more value in standard formats due to his knack for scoring touchdowns.

PROJECTION: 62 receptions 602 yards 6 TD

19. Tyler Eifert: The latest in a long-line of recent pass-catching Notre Dame tight ends to enter the NFL, Eifert had perhaps the most pub coming out of the draft after he was picked in the first round a year ago by the

Cincinnati Bengals. Unfortunately for Eifert and those who took him in fantasy football drafts, the presence of Jermaine Gresham served to take a machete to the rookie's numbers. Like in Philadelphia with Zach Ertz however, Eifert is the clear future at tight end for the Bengals and his pass-receiving skills are much more advanced then Gresham's are.

PROJECTION: 57 receptions 711 yards 5 TD

20. Coby Fleener: Much was expected out of Coby Fleener when he was selected in the second round of the 2012 draft to join college teammate Andrew Luck as prime components in the reinvented Indianapolis Colts offense. The thinking was that Fleener and Luck's chemistry would pick right back up in the NFL but instead fellow rookie Dwayne Allen became the top pass-receiving tight end. However with Allen missing most of 2013 with injury, Fleener finally showed what all the fuss was about by catching 52 balls for 608 yards and 4 touchdowns. Allen enters into 2014 with full health though so Fleener is likely to lose some of the numbers he compiled a year ago. Right now Fleener is best left as a bench option due to him and Allen siphoning stats from one another.

PROJECTION: 48 receptions 543 yards 4 TD

21. Dwayne Allen: As of press time third-year Indianapolis Colts tight end Dwayne Allen is taking part in OTA's as he is almost fully recovered from last year's hip surgery. It has been a long recovery back for Allen who suffered the injury in last year's opener, which was a big blow after he posted an intriguing 45 catches for 521 yards and 3 touchdowns as a rookie. Coby Fleener did an excellent job in his place last season and so Allen could now be behind his teammate in the passing game hierarchy as a result of his absence. Allen is really only worth drafting in standard formats due to his TD potential but even there he is looking like a shaky investment given Fleener's presence.

PROJECTION: 41 receptions 471 yards 4 TD

THE REST

22. Andrew Quarless: With Jermichael Finley out of the picture due to his neck injury and free agent status, up steps Andrew Quarless into the starting tight end spot. Any receiver who operates in the always explosive Packers passing attack deserves to be mentioned and on that front Quarless is at least semi-interesting. A bit stiff in his movements, Quarless is not capable of many big plays and has to have the ball thrown near his radius to make the catch. Little dynamics as far as ability is concerned but there is the possibility we could see 50 catches out of Quarless if all breaks right.

23. Levine Toilolo: With Tony Gonzalez now off into retirement, the starting tight end job falls to upstart Levine Toilolo. The fourth round pick of the 2013 draft was able to catch 2 touchdowns in limited time last season and no doubt he will see a whole lot more passing attention from Matt Ryan in 2014 with Gonzalez out of the picture. Worth a last round stab given the offense he plays in and his tight-end loving passer.

24. Jared Cook: Comes off a career-high 51 catches for 671 yards and 5 touchdowns but that is the ceiling of what Cook could do. Time to stop waiting for a breakout that is now not looking like it will ever arrive.

25. Owen Daniels: No longer fantasy football starting material now that he will back up the very capable Dennis Pitta in Baltimore. If Pitta gets hurt however, Daniels will be back in play.

26. Ryan Griffin: With Owen Daniels out of town, Griffin steps up as the number 2 tight end for the Houston Texans. Griffin has a nice combination of size, speed, and receiving skills so he could make some noise at some point. Monitor but don't draft.

27. Tim Wright: The rare WR/TE dual-eligible player last season, Wright was pretty useful as an undrafted rookie last season as he caught 54 balls for 571 yards and 5 touchdowns. The drafting of Austin Seferian-Jenkins removes some of the excitement from Wright's outlook however.

28. Jermichael Finley: A free agent as of this writing, Finley is trying to make his way back from a beyond scary neck injury suffered last season that ultimately required surgery. Before the injury Finley was an every week top ten tight end but until he finds a team and checks out medically, he is not worth looking into.

KICKERS

Draft Strategy: Nothing changes here as your kicker should be your very last pick in the draft. One of the most foolish moves you can make is to overdraft a kicker since they are pretty much a dime a dozen and the differences between them are very slight since they have to depend on the offense to put them in position to score.

1. Matt Prater
2. Stephen Gostowski
3. Justin Tucker
4. Steven Hauschka
5. Dan Bailey
6. Phil Dawson
7. Blair Walsh
8. Mason Crosby
9. Matt Bryant
10. Nick Novak
11. Robbie Gould
12. Greg Zuerlein
13. Graham Gano
14. Ryan Succup
15. Alex Henery
16. Shayne Graham

17. Adam Vinatieri

18. Caleb Sturgis

19. Sebastian Janikowski

20. Kai Forbath

21. David Akers

22. Jay Feely

23. Mike Nugent

24. Shaun Suisham

DEFENSE

Draft Strategy: Just as your kicker should be the last pick of the draft, your defense should be second-to-last. Streaming this spot is the way to go as it is once again almost impossible projecting on paper how potent a defense will be each season. Sure a splashy free agent signing or a prime draft pick could send a perceived defense's stock soaring. However we can bring you plenty of examples of top five defenses going into the season falling flat on their faces due to injuries, bad personnel mixtures, and just plain poor play. Way too tough to depend on these units as anything but late round picks.

1. Seattle Seahawks
2. San Francisco 49ers
3. Carolina Panthers
4. Cincinnati Bengals
5. Arizona Cardinals
6. St. Louis Rams
7. Denver Broncos
8. Kansas City Chiefs
9. New England Patriots
10. Baltimore Ravens
11. Chicago Bears
12. Pittsburgh Steelers
13. Tampa Bay Buccaneers
14. Green Bay Packers
15. Houston Texans

16. Buffalo Bills

17. Cleveland Browns

18. Miami Dolphins

19. New Orleans Saints

20. New York Jets

21. Philadelphia Eagles

22. New York Giants

23. Detroit Lions

24. Jacksonville Jaguars

25. Tennessee Titans

THE LAST WORD

As always it is good to keep in mind the fact that the draft is only the starting point to the season. The work towards building a league championship team is far from over and so following us all season long on The Fantasy Sports Boss (www.thefantasysportsboss.com) is the way to go. We will once again be on top of everything from constant injury updated on gameday to go along with features and profiles during the week to ensure your roster has the best chance of succeeding. In addition follow us on Twitter at RotoBoss as he tweet out news and notes all throughout the games each week. We look forward to helping you all reach your goal of securing victorious bragging rights in your league.

The Fantasy Sports Boss Staff
www.thefantasysportsboss.com
On Twitter at: RotoBoss

Made in the USA
Lexington, KY
08 June 2014